Health and Illness

SHORT INTRODUCTIONS

Published

Michael Bury, *Health and Illness*
Nicholas Abercrombie, *Sociology*
Robert W. Connell, *Gender*
Stephanie Lawson, *International Relations*

Forthcoming

Hartley Dean, *Social Policy*
Peter Dear and H. M. Collins, *Science*
Loraine Gelsthorpe, *Criminology*
Colin Hay, *Politics*
Christina Toren, *Anthropology*

Health and Illness

Michael Bury

polity

First published in 2005 by Polity Press

Polity Press
65 Bridge Street
Cambridge CB2 1UR, UK.

Polity Press
350 Main Street
Malden, MA 02148, USA

ISBN: 0-7456-3030-8
ISBN: 0-7456-3031-6 (pb)

A catalogue record for this book is available from the British Library.

Typeset in 10 on 12 pt Sabon
by SNP Best-set Typesetter Ltd, Hong Kong
Printed and bound in Great Britain by MPG Books Ltd, Bodmin, Cornwall

The publisher has used its best endeavours to ensure that the URLs for
external websites referred to in this book are correct and active at the time of
going to press. However, the publisher has no responsibility for the websites
and can make no guarantee that a site will remain live or that the content is
or will remain appropriate.

For further information on Polity, visit our website: www.polity.co.uk

Contents

What is Health?

Health is something of an enigma. Like the proverbial elephant, it is difficult to define but easy to spot when we see it. 'You look well' stands as a common greeting to a friend or a relative who appears relaxed, happy and buoyant – 'feeling good'. Any reflection on the term, however, immediately reveals its complexity. The idea of health is capable of wide and narrow application, and can be negatively as well as positively defined. We can be in good health and poor health. Moreover, health is not just a feature of our daily life, it also appears frequently on the political landscape. Health scares such as BSE/CJD, SARS and even the prospect of bio-terrorism have all exercised politicians and their medical advisers in recent times, and have all provided a steady stream of media stories. Health risks seem to proliferate, even if, for most of us most of the time, these are less than urgent concerns.

In all such instances, and in our more mundane experience, health is also related to other complex ideas such as illness and disease. This constellation of terms: health, disease and illness, and the experiences and forms of knowledge to which they relate, are the subjects of this opening chapter. In order to structure the discussion, the chapter is organized round four themes:

- The medical model of health and illness
- Lay concepts of health
- Health as attribute and health as relation
- Health and illness – physical and mental

These themes comprise substantive topics in their own right, but the discussion of them will also act as a lead into the subsequent chapters of the book. Many of the wider dimensions of health and illness – including their cultural and political features – will figure throughout the book. Examples of the most recent controversies in health are dealt with particularly in the latter stages. In this opening chapter, however, we need to begin with the basics and establish a conceptual map of the field.

The Medical Model of Health and Illness

On the surface it may seem somewhat perverse to begin a book on the sociology of health and illness by considering the medical model. However, given the importance, not to say dominance of medical science and medical practice in modern times, understanding the medical approach to health is a necessary starting point. Much of what contemporary populations think about health and illness, and much of the focus of research – including sociological research – is strongly influenced by the prevailing medical model. In public debate, the medical approach remains central. It is therefore with this topic that we begin.

It is often said that the medical model of health is a negative one: that is, that health is essentially the absence of disease. Despite bold attempts by bodies such as the World Health Organisation (WHO) to argue for a definition of health as 'a state of complete physical, mental and social well-being, and not merely the absence of disease or infirmity' (<www.who.int/about/overview/en>), most medically related thought remains concerned with disease and illness. This is hardly surprising, given the fact that people turn to medicine in times of trouble, not when they are feeling well. It has also been found that promotion of positive health, whether by doctors or 'health promoters', competes with other valued goals, for individuals and for societies as a whole. Matters become even more complicated when it is realized that the presence of 'disease or infirmity' does not, in any event, mean that people always regard themselves as unhealthy – as we shall see below. The phrase 'complete well-being' remains as elusive as it is positive, and health, illness and medicine are related in complex ways. The medical model of health, though often charged with 'reductionism', at least has the attraction of cutting through some of these knots.

As historians such as the late Roy Porter (2002a) have pointed out, the medical model, as we now know it, took on its main characteristics in the eighteenth and nineteenth centuries. Prior to this date most medicine in Western countries was committed to observation and the exhaustive classification of symptoms. Although this attachment to observation entailed a rejection of existing authorities (represented especially in Galen's writings) and was linked to a reformist view of science and society, developments were not straightforward. For many physicians in the seventeenth and eighteenth centuries, emerging views concerning the nature of disease were anathema. Physiology in France and chemistry in Germany were bringing the laboratory sciences to bear on human health and disease, and many thought this undermined the doctor's traditional role at the patient's bedside. However, during the nineteenth century, the development of bacteriology and pathological anatomy marked a major change in both thought and practice.

Instead of the seemingly endless classification of symptoms, the idea of 'specific aetiology' took hold, tracing the pathways of disease from underlying causes to pathology in human tissue or organ, and then to the manifestation of symptoms. Thus, specific causes were linked to specific diseases in particular organs, and the task of the physician was to trace the presenting symptoms back to their underlying origins. This model of disease flourished in the late nineteenth and early twentieth centuries, and was particularly associated with the discovery of the mechanisms that lay behind the infections – the so-called germ theory of disease. Although not all physicians, even then, as Porter (2002a) makes clear, accepted the idea of disease specificity, preferring to see sickness occurring when 'normal functions went awry' (p. 78), the pathologically based and causally specific medical model became increasingly dominant.

In order to illustrate what is meant here, let us take an example: the case of tuberculosis, an infectious disease responsible for a quarter of all deaths in the second half of the nineteenth century and the most important threat to health at that time (Webster 1994). In the medical model of disease, tuberculosis is defined as a disease of bodily organs (usually the lungs, but sometimes other sites such as the spine) following exposure to the tubercle bacillus. This exposure leads to pathological changes in the body's systems, and can be observed at x-ray as damage to the surface of the lungs, in the case of respiratory tuberculosis. The bacillus can be identified through culturing blood or sputum. The development of the illness involves symptoms such as coughing, haemoptysis (coughing up blood), weight loss and fever. In this model the underlying cause of the illness is the bacillus, and its elimination from the body (through anti-tubercular drugs) is aimed to restore the body to health. In 1944, streptomycin was found to be active against the tubercle bacillus.

The main point of this model of disease is that it attempts to uncover underlying pathological processes and their particular effects. The problem with earlier, symptom-oriented approaches to health was that no such sequences of events could be established, and treatment could only be symptomatic. In the case of tuberculosis, the symptoms described above are also found in other diseases, and this problem of linking symptoms to specific underlying mechanisms frustrated medical development. Fever, for example, is common to many infectious disorders. Once the specific aetiology approach was accepted, such symptomatic approaches were relegated to the margins of medicine. Although observation and the treatment of symptoms were established practices in early modern medicine, and have remained important to physicians ever since, it was often difficult to distinguish such approaches from a wide variety of unorthodox practices. Today, these are often referred to as forms of 'complementary medicine' – herbalism and homeopathy, for example – that treat symptoms 'holistically' – but do not rest on the idea of underlying, specific pathological disease mechanisms.

The medical historian Christopher Lawrence has argued that by 1920 in Britain, and in other developed countries such as the USA, the medical model, as outlined briefly above, had come to dominate medical thought and practice and, increasingly, society's attitude to health as a whole (Lawrence 1995). The medical model was essentially individualistic in orientation and, unlike earlier approaches, paid less attention to the patient's social situation or the wider environment. This narrowing of focus (towards the internal workings of the body, and then to cellular and sub-cellular levels), led to many gains in understanding and treatment, especially after 1941, when penicillin was introduced, and the era of antibiotics began. But it was also accompanied by the development of what Lawrence calls a 'bounded' medical profession, that could pronounce widely on health matters and could act with increasing power and autonomy. Doctors now claimed exclusive jurisdiction over health and illness, with the warrant of the medical model of disease as their support.

This situation meant that modern citizens were increasingly encouraged to see their health as an individual matter, and their health problems as in need of the attention of a doctor. It is this which Foucault (1973) saw as constituting the 'medical gaze' which focused on the individual and on processes going on inside the body – its 'volumes and spaces'. Wider influences on health, such as circumstances at work or in the domestic sphere, were of less interest to the modern doctor. This 'gaze' (extended in due course to health-related behaviours) underpinned the development of the modern 'doctor–patient' relationship, in which all authority over health matters was seen to reside in the doctors' expertise and skill, especially as shown in diagnosis. This meant that the patient's view of illness and alternative approaches to health were excluded from serious consideration. Indeed, the patient's view was seen as contaminating the diagnostic process, and it was better if the patient occupied only a passive role. It is for this reason that the 'medical model' of disease has been regarded critically in many sociological accounts. The power of the medical model and the power of the medical profession have been seen to serve the interests of 'medical dominance' rather than patients' needs (Freidson 1970/1988, 2001) and to direct attention away from the wider determinants of health.

However, before we proceed, two caveats need to be entered. Whilst medicine in the last 20 years has continued to focus on processes in the individual body, such as the chemistry of the brain or the role of genes in relation to specific diseases, the current context is clearly different from that which existed at the beginning of the twentieth century. Today, in countries such as the UK and the USA, infectious diseases are of far less importance as threats to human health. Though HIV/AIDS has become one of the most serious infectious diseases in history, its major impact is being felt in developing countries, especially in sub-Saharan Africa, and those of the former Soviet Union. In the West, notwithstanding the importance of infections when they do occur, the major health problems today are the so-called degenerative diseases associated with later life – conditions such as heart disease and cancer, and disabling illnesses such as arthritis and stroke. This has been referred to as the 'health transition' (Gray 2001: 127).

The medical model, today, therefore, is as likely to emphasize the complex or unknown aetiology of a disease as it is to discover its specific 'cause'. Many diseases can properly be recognized only by referring to a set of criteria (often arrived at by international groups of doctors) rather than identifying one underlying factor; diagnosis is often probabilistic rather than definitive. Treatment, in turn, may often be 'palliative', that is, trying to reduce the impact of symptoms, or contain the disease, rather than hoping to cure it completely. In addition, many doctors today work within multidisciplinary teams, rather than as isolated practitioners. They recognize (as the more thoughtful doctor has always done) the wider influences on health and the impact of disease on patients' lives. Indeed, the rhetoric currently surrounding 'patient partnership' and 'shared decision making', to be found in many developed health care systems, need not be treated entirely cynically. Many health care professionals are attempting to reshape health care to meet the new needs and demands of their patients. These changes need to be borne in mind as we look at the issues of medical power and the continuing influence of medical science later in this book.

Second, the individualistic approach to disease is not the only approach to health to be found in a more broadly defined medical model, though it may be the dominant one. Most developed societies have also had a long tradition of *public health*, focusing not on the individual but on the health of populations. Here, the diagnosis and treatment of individuals is less important than measures of health for whole groups and societies, however much these rely on medical scientific explanations of disease and illness. The most important of such measures are rates of mortality, morbidity and disability, data on which are collected and studied by the scientific arm of public health, epidemiology. Their regularity among and between groups of people is the focus of enquiry. As one leading UK epidemiologist has put it, epidemiology

> may be contrasted with the clinical observation of patients or the controlled experiment in the laboratory [as] the study of the health and disease of populations and groups in relation to their environment and ways of living . . . and is being applied to a variety of health services as well as health. (Morris 1975: 3)

Public health research, especially during the period dominated by the infections, was preoccupied with mortality data, especially the how, when and why of early death. For example, one of the most important measures of population health is the infant mortality rate (IMR), which calculates the number of deaths in the first year of life per thousand live births. Today the IMR for the UK is 5.5 and for the USA, is 6.8. However, the IMR for India is 63, and for Mali in West Africa, 121. Such statistics have been, and still are, an indication of the different life circumstances and health of the populations in these countries, in that high infant deaths are associated with poor maternal health and poor social circumstances. However, in Western countries, mortality statistics have become less sensitive indicators of population health as social conditions have improved (for mothers and other groups) and as the rates at all ages have continued to fall. None the less, as we shall see in chapter 2, much epidemiological research, and medical sociology work related to it, still rely on mortality data.

In recent years, though, public health and medical sociology have been concerned to develop more sensitive measures of health, still broadly within what one might call a 'socio-medical' model of health, but dealing with morbidity and disability (Bury 1997: 116). In such an approach, morbidity refers to measures of illness, and disability to measures of activity restriction and functional limitation, together with measures of quality of life. The important point to grasp at this stage is that the medical model contains a number of different strands of thought about human health, and different approaches to its study. This holds true, also, for the medical profession, which includes physicians, surgeons and general practitioners, together with public health doctors and epidemiologists. Whilst most medical practice has been individualistic in orientation, some forms of medicine (especially that focusing on human populations) have adopted a larger vision, and this often overlaps with sociological concerns. Medicine, like health, covers a wide range of phenomena and human activity, and this needs to be remembered when general statements about the 'medical model' or 'the medical profession' are made.

Lay Concepts of Health

If the above account of the growing dominance of the medical model is reasonably accurate, it might be expected that lay concepts of health in modern societies would be strongly influenced by it in modern times. Explanations for events such as illness are rarely couched, for example, in religious terms, at least not by the majority of lay people in countries such as the UK and the USA, though such ideas may be prevalent in particular communities. Medical information is disseminated and available in numerous ways today, especially through television, the Internet and other media. If the development of an individualistic medical model has shaped lay understanding and experience of health, then modern cultures have been equally conducive to its widespread acceptance. It would be surprising, under these circumstances, to find an entirely separate system of 'folk beliefs' about illness, shaped by a non-medical culture.

At the same time, enough has already been said to indicate that health, illness and medicine refer to a wide range of events and experiences, and ideas about these are bound to contain tensions and contradictions, as well as ambivalence about the role of medical treatments in dealing with them (Williams and Calnan 1996: 17). Sociological research on lay concepts of health has provided important insights into the complexity and sophistication of views about such matters. Whilst this work has shown the widespread absorption of medical messages about health, it has also shown how this is translated and reconciled with other areas of life, and assessed against alternative sources of information. Modern ideas about health and illness can also draw on earlier notions, such as the need for 'balance' in sustaining well-being.

In the first place it needs to be recognized that health may be an overriding concern to health care professionals and researchers, including medical sociologists, but not for lay people in everyday life. Health, for many, and for most of the time, is part of the 'natural attitude' to life, in which taken-for-granted meanings are an essential background and are unconsidered for much of the time. In his study of risk behaviour and HIV, Bloor (1995: 26), for example, drawing on the writings of Alfred Schutz, distinguished between 'the world of routine activities' and 'a world of considered alternatives and calculative action' in interpreting how health risks were perceived by his respondents. Bloor's study reinforces the view that daily life presupposes health, unless it is threatened by events or information that draw the layperson into considering alternatives. Health risks vie with the routine nature of daily life, with its own pressures and pleasures, constraints and potentialities. As we shall see below, only a minority of people are forced, or choose, to abandon an assumption of health as a given. Those concerned with health promotion (as opposed to the treatment of illness) who wish to encourage lay people to become more health-conscious have to face this issue in doing so. Health is not necessarily a pressing and overriding value, consciously considered on a daily basis. Information on health risks is actively interpreted within specific social contexts (Alaszweski and Horlick-Jones 2003).

In addition to this, lay thinking about the causes or origins of good and ill health has been found to be characterized by complex considerations. Even if health is often taken for granted, and only missed when it is felt to be compromised, this does not mean that lay people lack clear ideas about the relationship between health and illness. In one of the earliest and most influential studies of lay concepts of health, Herzlich (1973) showed how, among a sample of 80 middle-class French respondents (mostly from Paris) health was linked to the connections between individuals and 'the way of life'. Health beliefs, or the 'representations of health' as Herzlich called them, located the source of illness in the character of urban living, with its tendency to create stress, fatigue and nervous tension. This, it was felt, could 'facilitate' or 'release' forces that could aid the development of illness. But such forces could also 'generate' illness – that is, be more pathological in their own right – and not just exacerbate existing problems, for example, by making an infection worse.

Positive health, on the other hand, was seen to be inherent in the individual. The balance or 'equilibrium' between the healthy individual and illness could be upset by a number of features of the environment. Cancer was linked to allergies, and to the nervous strain of city life and the polluted atmosphere found there. Mental illness was linked to the 'restlessness' of modern living, and heart disease to the 'many worries which make people live in a certain state of anxiety' (Herzlich 1973: 22). Whilst the respondents in this study recognized that individual attributes might contribute to poor health, these attributes were never seen as both necessary and sufficient. The individual's 'nature', heredity, temperament or predisposition might make the individual vulnerable, but the 'way of life' remained crucial to the development of poor health.

If Herzlich's work set out to provide a framework for understanding the links between way of life and the individual in lay concepts of health, subsequent work has explored their variation across different age and social groups. In a study which builds conceptually on Herzlich, but draws on a large national study of health and lifestyles in the UK, Blaxter (1990) has provided a detailed picture of some of these variations. This study also shows that health is not a single or unitary concept, but one that has a number of dimensions as applied to different areas of life and lifestyles (see also Blaxter 2003, 2004).

Blaxter's (1990) discussion of lay beliefs is drawn from responses to open-ended questions about health put to 9,000 respondents in England, Wales and Scotland. Overall, these responses show that for lay people 'health can be defined negatively, as the absence of illness, functionally as the ability to cope with everyday activities, or positively as fitness and well-being' (p. 14). However, there are two important additions to this general picture. The first is that health has a moral dimension, reflecting not only the adoption or maintenance of a healthy lifestyle, but also how people respond to illness and deal with its aftermath. Illness runs the risk of devaluing a person's identity, either because of its causation (e.g. smoking, sexual contact, failure to 'keep well') or because of inappropriate behaviour in the face of symptoms. Moral dimensions of health have been found in a number of other studies, such as Conrad's (1994) study of students in the USA and G. Williams's (1984) study of middle-aged and older people with arthritis in England. From this viewpoint illness is not simply a deviation from biological norms, as in the medical model, but a significant departure from social norms.

Second, Blaxter shows that health, illness and disease are not always mutually exclusive in lay thought. Respondents in her study often reported that they saw themselves as healthy despite having serious conditions such as diabetes. There is clearly a strong motivation towards feeling and being seen to be healthy, if at all possible. This issue becomes particularly salient when the question of disability is considered, given the complex relationship between health and a range of different disabling conditions. For individuals with stable disabilities, or conditions that are not accompanied by generalized illness or 'malaise', being healthy may be redefined to incorporate how the person feels now, not in relation to a general norm. Adaptation to illness or disability alters the baseline from which the individual judges the nature of health and its implications. As we shall see below, however, and in more detail in chapter 4, the relationship between disability and health has become highly controversial.

One of the main strengths of Blaxter's study is that it shows the importance of gender and age to such definitions of health. Blaxter argues that health in much lay thinking can be seen to constitute a form of 'reserve stock', to be invested in by adopting healthy behaviours, or diminished by self-neglect or unhealthy behaviours (Blaxter 1990: 16). The 'health capital' we are born with can be seen as a function of heredity and as being shaped by development in the early years of life. But people in later life may feel that their 'stock' is diminishing or running down. Problems with mobility, eyesight and hearing are obvious examples. In Blaxter's study older people did, indeed, report more negative views of their health, with men under the age of 40 more likely to emphasize a positive notion of 'fitness'. Health as functioning – being able to carry out self-care and other routine tasks – is likely to increase in importance with age, and likewise is largely taken for granted among the young. For young women, however, Blaxter's study underlined the importance of social relationships, as well as being patient with children and 'coping with the family' (Blaxter 1990: 27).

In Blaxter's study, then, the nuanced and multidimensional character of lay health beliefs is underlined. This is of particular note, especially in a period when health risks appear to be multiplying. For example, fears have been expressed that the 'new genetics' will overwhelm modern populations with burdensome information about potential health risks and the need to make choices about an ever wider range of medical and health-promoting interventions (including screening programmes). The incorporation of an increasing number of human and social problems into the medical and genetic orbit has led sociologists to analyse the various forces, concerns and dilemmas involved (Conrad 2000). Even, here, though, empirical research has found that lay people are able to absorb or deal with even the most technical and complex information in creative and practical ways. A brief example to conclude this section of the chapter can serve to illustrate the point.

As part of an ongoing programme of research at Cardiff University, Parsons and Atkinson (1992) reported on the knowledge and beliefs of 22 mothers and 32 daughters who had a known risk of carrying the gene responsible for Duchenne muscular dystrophy, a disease that leads, slowly, to a progressive degeneration of muscular tissue. It is inherited through a recessive, sex-linked gene, so that only boys are affected, and only women can pass it on. There is no effective treatment for the disease, and the outlook for many affected individuals, in the medium term, is poor. It might be expected that under these circumstances reproductive decisions on the part of the women in the study would be likely to be highly problematic. Each woman in the study had gone through several assessments and tests, resulting, finally, in two sets of risk figures, one for her carrier status and one for her risk of passing on the gene to any offspring. In fact, Parsons and Atkinson found considerable confusion on the part of some women as to the nature of the statistics they had been given. However, the point of the study was not to demonstrate the women's ability to account for their carrier status, or otherwise, but to explore how the knowledge they did have was incorporated into daily life. Parsons and Atkinson found that the women had invariably trans-lated statistical risk into 'descriptive categories that had become routine recipes for their reproductive behaviour', so that specific figures could be seen, for example, as putting them at high or low risk of transmission (Parsons and Atkinson 1992: 441). Far from being disempowered by expert knowledge, the women were able to use these descriptive state-ments to inform action, in ways that the medical information could not. Probabilistic knowledge derived from genetics was turned into more certain guidelines that could deal with both decision making and social relationships. For much of the time the women were able to relegate their carrier status to a 'low zone of relevance'. In this study health beliefs were shown not only as sophisticated but also as practical, being fash-ioned and refashioned as contexts and experiences changed. As we saw earlier, health beliefs are integrated, where possible, into the routine actions that constitute everyday life.

This is not to say that all lay health beliefs are true or unproblematic. While medical sociology has made an important contribution to under-standing the rationality, relevance and socially contextualized nature of lay health beliefs, it is important not to overstate the argument. Whilst individuals have unique insights into their own situations, these cannot be substituted for expert knowledge in all and every circumstance (Prior 2003). The economist Amartya Sen (2002) has shown, for example, that when a comparative perspective of lay views is adopted, anomalies quickly appear. Quoting data from India and the USA, he shows that the higher the level of education in a population, the higher the level of reported illness. This stands in contrast to more 'objective' measures, such as mortality rates and life expectancy, which, as indicated earlier in this chapter, are much more favourable in the USA than in a country such as India. We should not conclude from their stated beliefs or behav-iours that people in the USA are less healthy than people in India. Rather, we should see lay beliefs and behaviour, as well as the medical model, as components of a dialectic, interacting in complex ways, and mediated by different cultural settings.

Health as Attribute and Health as Relation

The previous two sections have explored, in outline, the medical model and lay beliefs about health. One of the ways we can think sociologi-cally about the tension between the two is to consider health in terms of attribute and relation. The relationship between these two approaches also provides us with a framework with which to approach some of the most puzzling features of contemporary health phenomena.

If we take the idea of attribute first, much medical knowledge, and considerable areas of lay belief influenced by it, make the assumption that disease or illness is a property or attribute of the individual. Disease from this viewpoint is an 'it' which the person has or harbours. In early modern medicine it was often felt that scientific investigation ran the risk of 'reifying' disease – that is, of creating a 'thing' separate from the individual patient, where only observed symptoms could properly be identified. Humoral medicine treated disease and its symptomatology as one and the same. With the ascendancy of the 'pathological anatomy' perspective, 'reified' disease became increasingly dominant. In this new view, disease was seen as a separate entity, both from the attempts to conceptualize it or deal with it, and from the symptoms that might or might not be related to it. Diseases such as tuberculosis, and bodily organs such as lungs, exist, in this realist view, whether we name them or not, or whether we live in a culture or a period of history which has a different understanding. Moreover, many diseases exist without symptoms, especially in their early stages – in some forms of heart disease and cancer, for example. And the plethora of observable symptoms often do not map on to disease in a one-to-one manner. The existence of cultures (or histories) that do not conceptualize disease as an independent property of the body does not mean that people do not have diseases or organs such as lungs, hearts or livers (Craib 1995). Though diseases may be caused by outside agents (bacteria, viruses), their essential character reside in the human body, as an attribute of its physical make-up.

A relational view of health, by contrast, does not focus on the biological determinants at work in the individual's body. Rather, it points to the social or psycho-social forces that influence the pattern and expression of illness. This can be conceptualized in two ways: either in terms of the 'social creation' of illness patterns through inequalities or environmental factors, or in terms of the 'social production' of illness in individuals through the contingencies and negotiations that surround its identification, naming and treatment. This latter approach is especially relevant to forms of chronic illness (Gerhardt 1989). Here, the process of recognizing or naming a disease, by medical staff or lay people, involves a range of factors, including the severity of symptoms, the age and tolerance level of the sufferer, the social circumstances of the individual (work or family difficulties, for example), and the interactions between the person and the health care system. Many chronic conditions are difficult to separate from the normal, again, especially in their early stages, and there may not be a key hallmark, comparable with a bacterium or virus, that can act as a definitive marker for the disease. In this sense the disease or illness may be 'negotiated' before a definite name or plan of action is agreed upon.

At this point, it may be thought that an attributional view of health is largely the province of medicine and the medical model of health, and a relational view that of lay people or, indeed, of the sociologist. In many situations this may well be the case, but again the idea of dialectic is important. Take the case of a disease such as osteoarthritis, a common disorder of later life, involving progressive deterioration in the joints of the body, especially the hips. As the disease is associated with age, many people tend to discount the aches and pains which accompany it as features of growing older, and treat them as more or less normal. Or, at least, it has been found that people attempt to do so (Sanders et al. 2002). Thus, reporting of such symptoms to the doctor is likely to be highly variable. At the same time, the fit between symptoms and degree of disease progression is often difficult for doctors to judge. Patients with low levels of pain may have badly affected joints, and those in considerable pain may not show signs of major physical changes (for example, at x-ray). How the severity of the disease is judged, and whether or when to intervene (for example, by surgical replacement of a hip), is, in part at least, a matter for negotiation. It may be contingent on a host of factors, not least the presence of a waiting list for surgery.

In this respect the medical view of disease cannot easily operate within an entirely attributional perspective. Returning to our earlier point, and as Healy (1999: 12) has pointed out, the 'specific disease model' of the late nineteenth century overcame earlier confusions created by a form of medicine which relied on a combination of theory and observation. Healy cites the case of diphtheria in this period, which was often confused with other throat problems, and only resolved when a specific diphtheria organism was isolated. To repeat, the new medical model emphasized that specific causes gave rise to specific diseases. Whilst this may still hold true for some diseases today, the rise in importance of degenerative conditions requires that medical knowledge and medical practice often adopt a 'multi-factorial' model of illness, wherein physical, psychological and social processes are recognized as playing an important part. Even where genetic knowledge is giving renewed impetus to the specific cause approach, it is recognized that genes may express themselves in different ways in different individuals and within different environments.

By the same token, a relational view of health is not always characteristic of lay views. An attributional view of disease has, in recent years, become highly attractive among some lay people, especially in connection with problematic and contentious disorders. The 'way of life' may not always be the main emphasis in lay thinking about disease causation. Conditions such as Attention Deficit Hyperactivity Disorder (ADHD), Myalgic Encephalomyelitis (ME) or Chronic Fatigue Syndrome (CFS), and Gulf War Syndrome are among the best publicized in this regard. ME/CFS is held by many sufferers to be the result of a viral illness, and not, as many doctors think, the outcome of psychological problems including depression. The paradox lies in the fact that it is patients, and not doctors, who are claiming that the illness results from an underlying biological attribute, and it is doctors who are warning against the 'medicalization' of 'non-diseases', fuelled by genetics on the one hand and an expansionist pharmaceutical industry on the other (Moynihan and Smith 2002). Claims made about the 'objective' or 'real' nature or causes of a disorder do not themselves, of course, mean that they are true.

Nevertheless, the attraction for many lay people of regarding a condition such as ME/CFS as a biological attribute seems unstoppable. The UK organization Action for ME states, for example, that the disorder is a 'potentially chronic and disabling neurological disorder, which causes profound exhaustion, muscle pain and cognitive problems such as memory loss and concentration . . . it is estimated that around two thirds of all cases are preceded by a viral infection of some kind' (Action for ME, <www.afme.org.uk>). Activists in areas such as this can become hostile to arguments, especially from medical sources that fail to share such an approach. To repeat, ME/CFS is only one among a number of health problems which express a complex relationship between attributional and relational issues, that do not necessarily follow the disease = medical, illness = lay distinction.

If we bring disability into the picture again, these problems are thrown into sharp relief. As G. Williams (2000) has noted, for most doctors and lay people the idea of disability has been as a 'property' of the individual. Impairments resulting from disease or trauma, that alter the structure or functioning of the body, become disabling. By this is meant that the affected individual has difficulty or is unable to perform the usual tasks that a non-impaired person would be able to carry out, such as self-care or mobility. The causal chain of disease/trauma → impairment → disability reproduces the essential characteristics of the medical model described earlier. This attributional view of disability has dominated not only medical thought, but also lay understanding. Indeed, without it, it would be difficult to make any assessment of the degree of disability or to allocate resources (for example, designated parking places or disability allowances) with any degree of fairness. If it is not possible to distinguish between the able-bodied and the disabled in attributional terms, then such issues become almost impossible to resolve.

In recent years, however, radical voices in the disability movement have sought to separate disease, impairment and the body, on the one hand, from disability, on the other. In this view disability is wholly relational, in that it is seen to be a product of social oppression and discrimination (Oliver 1996: 35). The idea of disability being a property or attribute of the individual has become anathema to some, and its essentially relational character a test of radical disability credentials. Considerable argument has ensued about the nature of disability between these two poles, both within the disability movement and between disability activists and medical sociologists (Bury 1996; Shakespeare 1999). G. Williams notes that sociologists such as Irving Zola (who was himself disabled) have argued that moving too far in either the relational or the attributional direction oversimplifies the complex problems involved. Instead, Zola favoured a formulation widely used in the USA: namely, that of referring to 'people with disabilities' (G. Williams 2000: 139; Zola 1993), recognizing both the bodily and the social dimensions at work.

These issues will be returned to in greater detail in chapter 4 of this book. The main point to note here is that in the field of health and illness, and in areas such as psychosomatic disorders or disability, a tension between attributional and relational aspects is inevitably present. A critical sociological view of health has at its centre the dialectic of physical and social dimensions. This is not the same, however, as arguing that health and illness are merely 'social constructs', in the sense that they depend only on shifting social contexts and different interests at work. The difficulties with a sociological view that gives no place to the biological and 'embodied' character of health is that it leaves the body and its make-up (especially in the current period, its genetic make-up) to medical scrutiny alone. To argue that health has a social dimension is not to say that it has no independent or physical basis; nor is it to argue that medical knowledge is little more than the exercise of unwarranted power over the layperson. Some disorders are controversial and difficult to define, others are not. In some circumstances physical symptoms inexorably overwhelm the individual's body, in others they are recognized only through a more negotiated process. Indeed, these different aspects of experience will often unfold in varying ways in the course of a particular illness. How perceptions, experience and action work their way through in specific disorders is a matter for empirical analysis. This book will suggest that a *dynamic* view of health is needed, one in which changes over time (across the individual lifecourse, and in different societies at different historical periods) become the focus of analysis. In such a view, attribute and relation are necessary concepts for a full understanding of health.

Health and Illness – Physical and Mental

Up to this point the discussion has been largely concerned with physical health and physical illness or disability. Indeed, much of this short book will necessarily be confined to physical health and illness. None the less, this introductory discussion cannot properly conclude without considering, if only briefly, the difficult issues presented by mental health.

In recent years, as Busfield (2000) has pointed out in a useful review, developments in genetics, neuroscience and pharmacology have tended to reinforce a perspective of mental health as being determined by bodily processes – what here has been called an attributional view. The idea that mental health is a product of the individual's biological make-up has proved attractive to lay people as well to those in medicine in many different periods of history. A materialist – not to say mechanical – view of the body, and especially the brain with its structures, linkages and chemistry, has dominated medical and psychiatric thought since early modern times, following the rejection of 'demonic' and religious-based explanations of mental disturbance. Developments in psychology, and the influence of thinking such as Freud's on the role of early development and fantasy in human affairs, have not displaced the desire among most psychiatrists to remain in the medical mainstream. Not surprisingly, therefore, a medical model of mental health has continued to be influential in lay cultures. The apparent neutrality of the medical model also has its attractions. As with other forms of illness, to be told that a mental disorder is the result of an organic disturbance provides a way of resisting claims that it may result from a failure of character or from a weak will.

Indeed, one of the main difficulties with mental illness is that it often involves changes in behaviour which attract moral opprobrium. Strange, difficult or threatening behaviour, as Fabrega and Manning (1973) and Goffman (1971) argued over 30 years ago, reflect on the selfhood of the putative patient and create interactional difficulties. In physical ill health it is often possible to distance oneself from the disorder in question by appealing to independent influences such as germs or viruses, or to other non-motivational factors. As was shown above, however, concepts of health and illness often carry moral connotations; even a simple infection such as influenza may be thought to be the result of self-neglect, and more serious illnesses are often linked to poor lifestyle choices such as smoking or over-indulgence in food or alcohol. Nevertheless, mental health is particularly prone to negative judgements, because the very definition of the problem is linked to the person's self or behaviour. For an individual to say that they cannot work because of an infection or other more serious physical illness is, even today, quite different from disclosing the presence, for example, of depression or psychosis. The latter illnesses almost always raise questions about the individual and their personality (including the risk of dangerous or disturbing behaviour), and this contrasts strongly with disclosures of physical illness. It is no wonder, then, that an 'attributional' view, which locates mental illness in the person's biological make-up, has proved attractive to professional and lay audiences alike, even though this may only reduce rather than eliminate negative reactions.

By the same token, approaching mental health in relational terms – in terms of interpersonal and social processes – does not always find favour in professional *or* lay circles. Studies of the family dynamics of mental illness in the 1960s appeared only to end up 'blaming the victim' – in this case the families caring for seriously mentally ill individuals. Yet, psycho-social theories and the social circumstances of many of those suffering from mental health problems provide a continuing basis for sociological research and policy. As Busfield (2000) makes clear, sociology has had, and continues to have, much to contribute to the understanding of mental health by examining its social dimensions. Following the discussion in the last section, it is possible to distinguish the role of the social in the 'creation' or causation of mental illness, from its 'social production' – that is, the expression and definition of the illness and the way it unfolds in social interaction.

As Busfield states, there is a long history of social and epidemiological research on the creation or occurrence of mental illness. Whilst this has sometimes been criticized by sociologists for taking the medical definition of illness (or 'mental disease') as given, much of the work has challenged the individualistic orientation of psychiatric thought. In early pioneering studies in the USA, Faris and Dunham (1965 [1939]) and Hollingshead and Redlich (1958) attempted to show that mental disorder was not a random event, dependent solely on the individual's biological characteristics, but was patterned by social circumstances (including poverty) and social class. In this way, mental health has been located as an aspect of health inequalities (Rogers and Pilgrim 2003), showing that its occurrence is significantly determined by social factors. However, debates concerning the role of factors such as ethnicity and racism in serious mental illnesses such as schizophrenia (Littlewood and Lipsedge 1997; Kelleher and Hillier 1996) vie with evidence indicating their universality across social groups. This indicates that social influences on their causation are open to doubt (Hafner and an der Heiden 1997) and require careful assessment.

One of the difficulties in explaining mental disorder is that much of it is hidden. At any one time the number of people being treated is only a fraction of those living with undiagnosed illness in the community. If the study of mental illness concentrates on those already in contact with the services, little can be said about its origins, unless a clear account can be given of the selection process that has led some to receive treatment and some not. Moreover, social conditions may change between the onset of a disorder and making contact with services, acting as a further confounding factor. Although the US studies, mentioned above, tried to estimate this effect, large-scale epidemiological studies in the community are difficult and expensive to mount (and run the risk of creating large estimates of illness which fuel the 'medicalization' of whole communities, and provide new markets for the pharmaceutical companies). In Britain, one of the best-known studies of mental disorder in the community (in this case, depression) attempted to control for the possible confounding factors involved by making rigorous assessments of the circumstances surrounding the onset of illness among community-based samples (Brown and Harris 1978). This study challenged prevailing definitions of depression by showing that severe life events involving loss and threat had a major impact on the onset and development of depression, in the presence of vulnerability factors such as early loss of a mother, low socio-economic status and the lack of a confiding relationship. Subsequent work in this tradition has shown that neglect and abuse in childhood also have a significant influence on the occurrence of adult depression, indicating that genetic influences are unlikely to be a major determining factor in this disorder (Bifulco and Moran 1998).

As far as the 'social production' or shaping of mental health is concerned, a number of important studies, especially in the USA during the 1960s and 1970s, employed a deviancy perspective to try to explain the medicalization of disturbing and distressing behaviours in terms of illness. Perhaps the best-known study of this period is Scheff's *Being Mentally Ill* (1999 [1967]). Scheff's argument, essentially, revolved round two key concepts. The first of these is 'residual deviance', which, he argued, helps explain the wide variety of disorders and conditions which are held to make up mental illness. 'Residual deviance' is essentially behaviour which is found to be unacceptable, but which is not categorized in other ways, such as being regarded as criminal. This approach to mental illness draws heavily on labelling theory, in that the behaviour designated as mental illness is that which attracts the label. Behaviour so labelled in one time or place might not be so labelled in another time or place. Goffman (1963a) famously pointed to the example of praying. Being on one's knees in a praying posture is acceptable in a designated religious building, but not on the street outside. The contexts and contingencies surrounding particular problems help explain their labelling, or otherwise. Homosexuality, once regarded as a mental disorder by psychiatry, is not regarded as such now, having been voted out of psychiatric classifications by American and British psychiatrists in the 1970s. In such ways mental illness can be produced, or not, depending on social contingencies.

Second, Scheff argued that 'societal reaction' to residual deviance helps explain the *career* of mental health patients. Once labelled, the individual is likely to take on the characteristics of the label, thus confirming the original social response. Like Goffman (1963b), Scheff saw that identity could be powerfully influenced, and indeed spoiled, by one characteristic of the individual being generalized to their whole self. The stigma of mental illness, as a diagnosis, could have real effects, independently of any underlying disorder. Institutional 'warehousing' of psychiatric patients in large mental hospitals, which had come to dominate the pattern of care during the twentieth century, seems to have served only to reinforce this process. Though critics such as Gove (1974) argued that negative societal reaction was the last, rather than the first, resort of families and communities to disturbing behaviour, Scheff's work, along with other 'anti-psychiatry' arguments at the time, provided a powerful challenge to social and professional attitudes towards mental illness.

In recent years, the writings of Foucault (1967, 1973) have been used to supplement and reinforce a critical view of psychiatry, medicine and social control, in 'producing' mental illness. For Foucault, the control of mental illness was expressed by the 'great confinement' in eighteenth- and nineteenth-century France, leading to the repression of 'unreason' and the policing of troublesome and threatening behaviour. Here the state and the medical profession were seen as treating mentally ill people as excluded from the world of reason, and consigning large numbers of them to the degrading conditions of mental hospitals. However, as Porter (2002b) has argued, such a picture is simplistic and over-generalized, especially when applied to other countries such as the USA and UK, where hospitalization of the mentally ill was on a relatively small scale until the end of the nineteenth century. Porter also shows that a number of vested interests (and safeguards) were at work in shaping responses to mental illness, though he also sees that by the Second World War many large hospitals had 'degenerated into sites dominated by formal drills, financial stringency, and drug routines' (p. 120), with some 150,000 inmates being in such institutions in Britain in 1950. Their numbers had dropped to some 30,000 by the 1980s (p. 211).

It is somewhat paradoxical, perhaps, that attempts to 'de-institutionalize' the mentally ill in the last 20 years have gone hand in hand with a renewed emphasis on the biology and genetics of mental health, as much as on its 'relational' character. One way in which this paradox is explicable is, of course, to be found in the widespread use of anti-psychotic, anti-depressive and anxiolytic drugs. Though based on chemical and neurological theories of mental illness, they have effectively 'dampened down' symptoms and made patients relatively more manageable in the community. The pharmacological revolution in psychiatry has been married with policies to develop widespread forms of 'community care'. Whether this counts as a more effective way of treating the mentally ill and helps to reduce its 'production' or has led to a more tolerant view of mental health problems is a matter of judgement rather than hard evidence. The ability of people in different social contexts to tolerate and respond positively to a range of illness states is clearly contingent on many factors, including the degree of disruption of social interaction they involve and the level of tolerance of families, workmates and wider communities. Nevertheless, mental health continues to present particular difficulties, especially when people 'translate disgust into the disgusting and fears into the fearful' (Porter 2002b: 62). The distinctions between social responses to mental illness and physical illness raised here remain powerful ones and need to be borne in mind in discussions about health.

Concluding Remark

Health can be seen as a multifaceted dimension of human life, and as a 'reserve stock' (Blaxter 2003, 2004) of vitality, fitness and strength (whether psychological or physical or both) which individuals can draw upon to pursue their goals and actions. From a sociological viewpoint health can be seen as both 'attribute' and 'relation', simultaneously involving biological and social factors. This suggests a *dynamic* view of health and illness, changing across biographical and historical time. The experience of health, both good and poor, is likely to be influenced by the circumstances into which people are born and the contexts and actions which prevail at different stages of life. Health and illness thus take us to a crucial intersection of biography and history. The social patterning of health which results from this intersection is the focus of the next chapter.

2

The Patterning of Health and Illness

It is an axiom of medical sociology that health is both personal and social in character. In the terms of the discussion in the last chapter, health can be seen as both attributional and relational. Viewed from a personal point of view, health and illness can take on intense existential and practical meanings, and it is these with which individuals are most often concerned. The onset of a serious, life-threatening disorder, or one which carries the risk of significant disability, can disrupt a person's physical well-being and simultaneously his or her relationships with others; attribute and relation interact in many different ways. Behind much of the academic discussion of health, therefore, lie the symptoms, distress and pain of individual lives. At the same time, it is clear that health has important social dimensions, including the fact that many, if not most, disorders do not occur randomly in populations. They are, in significant ways, socially patterned.

This chapter aims to provide an overview of what has, by now, become a very large literature of the social patterning of health. The sociology of health and illness has made significant contributions to the study of health inequalities in particular, and much of what it has to say on this subject overlaps with the medical public health perspective discussed in the last chapter. At other points, inequalities research touches on psychological aspects of health – for example, in the area of stress. Because of the range and extent of work on the social patterning of health, the chapter is organized round four main themes. The first part of the chapter tackles the issues of health inequalities, especially in relation to social class – what in the USA is often referred to as 'socio-economic status' (SES). Second, the chapter discusses the question of health and the life-course, and especially the debate about the 'Barker hypothesis', which posits strong influences of circumstances at birth, and in early life, on health in adult life. Third, the chapter provides a discussion of ethnicity and health, in which the complex relationships between ethnic status and other social factors are explored. Finally, a note is provided on the level of analysis to be found in research on social patterning, and attempts to overcome an overly individualistic view by exploring the role of 'place' in current sociological enquiry on health. The important issue of gender is held over for discussion in its own right in chapter 3.

Health Inequalities and Social Class

It is possible to identify two broad perspectives within the health inequalities literature: a materialist or structural perspective, on the one hand, and a social cohesion, or psycho-social perspective, on the other. Though these can be distinguished in a general overview of the literature, it is worth noting that they often overlap in particular pieces of work. In the UK, the structural or materialist perspective has been particularly associated in the last 20 years or so with the 'Black Report' and the debate that has surrounded its publication and aftermath. The report, commissioned in the late 1970s by the then Labour government (and named after the chairman of the Research Working Group which produced it, Sir Douglas Black), was published in 1980, and later reprinted and expanded (Townsend and Davidson 1992). In this report, the authors surveyed the situation with respect to health inequalities in Britain, using data that covered the 25-year period from the setting up of the National Health Service (NHS) in 1948, up to the early 1970s.

As mentioned in the previous chapter, one of the most important measures of population health is mortality rates, especially those on 'premature mortality' which reveal who survives and who succumbs to early death. The main part of the Black Report was concerned with linking mortality data with occupational social class, taken as a crucial indicator of social position and status. Social class, at this time, was measured using the Registrar General's classification of occupations, which was readily available for epidemiological and sociological analysis (see end-of-chapter note). The adoption of this approach to measuring social position was, according to the report, a largely pragmatic one: 'we shall employ occupation as a basis of class because of its convenience' (Townsend and Davidson 1992: 40). The mortality data used focused on a number of measures, though two are of particular significance: infant mortality (deaths in the first year of life) and premature adult mortality (deaths among those aged 15–64). The impact of the report stemmed from two main findings with respect to these measures.

The first of these concerned infant mortality. The Working Group found, on the basis of data for 1970–2, that 'for the death of every one male infant of professional parents, we can expect almost two among children of skilled manual workers and three among children of unskilled manual workers. Among females the ratios are even greater' (Townsend and Davidson 1992: 44). The report found that deaths from accidents and respiratory disease showed the most marked class gradient. These are causes of death which, the authors argue, are closely related to the 'socio-economic environment', and which constitute major risks to health in the early months of life. Respiratory disease in infants, for example, might relate to the physical condition of the home (including such factors as dampness) and to behaviours such as smoking, which is more common in poorer families.

As far as adult mortality is concerned, the report relied heavily on the use of 'standardized mortality ratios' (SMRs), which compare the experience of a particular subgroup with the average for the group as a whole (in this case a particular social class subgroup compared with mortality rates for all males or females aged 15–64). The average rate for the group as a whole, against which subgroups can be compared, is given the value of 100. In examining SMRs in this way, an inverse relationship appears. The higher the social class, the lower the mortality, and the lower the social class, the higher the mortality. To illustrate the point, the authors state that 'the mortality ratio for former miners and quarrymen was 149 [that is 49 points above, or worse than the average], gas, coke and chemical makers 150, and furnace, forge, foundry and rolling mill workers 162. By comparison, administrators and managers had SMRs of 88, and professional technical workers and artists 89 [that is, 22 and 21 per cent respectively lower, or better than the average]' (Townsend and Davidson 1992: 48). Again, in the report, the causes of death for those workers experiencing high levels of mortality relate to the impact of material and structural factors, such as poor or dangerous working conditions. Diseases such as those of the respiratory system show a particularly strong social class gradient for adults, with much higher levels among manual workers than those in professional groupings.

More recent data on mortality and social class in the UK have appeared to reinforce the picture painted by the Black Report. Drever and Whitehead (1997), for example, using data for the period 1991–3 have shown that SMRs for men between the ages of 20 and 64 continue to show large differences by social class. Deaths from all causes produce an overall SMR of 66 for social class I (that is, 34 points lower than the average) and 189 for unskilled manual workers (that is, 89 points above the average) (Drever and Whitehead 1997: 98). Infant mortality is also still marked by social class inequalities, with particularly high rates for infants born outside marriage (p. 86). It is important to note here that while mortality has been the main focus of debates about health inequalities, significant social gradients in health status have also been found using measures of illness or morbidity, self-assessed health (Blaxter 1990) and disability (Arber and Ginn 1991). Thus, the Black Report and subsequent data from other sources have revealed persisting inequalities in health in the UK which seem, if anything, to be worsening over time. It is equally important to note, however, that this evidence is about the *relative* position of different social groups – in the examples discussed here, different social classes. This does not mean that overall health in the population has worsened. Quite the reverse: it has improved considerably with each passing decade since 1945. With few exceptions mortality rates have improved – that is, fallen – at all ages, especially in the last 20 years. General health improvement can therefore occur alongside persisting and even widening inequalities.

Having said this, significant patterning of health by social position has been found in many other developed (as well as underdeveloped) countries. Mortality data from a range of different countries have been linked with differences in material circumstances. In the USA, for example, income and education levels have been widely used as measures of social position, or 'socio-economic status' (SES), rather than occupational social class. Link and Phelan (2000), for example, have noted that in the USA 'people at the bottom of the education and income distributions are at two to three times greater risk of dying [early] than those at the top of the distributions' (p. 38). Explanations given for these inequalities in terms of individual risk factors (such as smoking or diet) fail on their own 'to explain the persistence of the SES association'. Instead, these authors point to what they argue is the ability of people with more resources to avoid hazards to health more easily, and to take advantage of protective devices (better health care or moving to a more conducive environment). The social conditions that promote or inhibit risks to health are termed by Link and Phelan 'fundamental social causes' (p. 38).

Although these arguments, developed by both UK and US researchers, tend to reject explanations for health patterning based on individual behaviours that carry health risks, and thus avoid blaming the victims, their arguments raise some important questions. These point to dimensions of health risks that go beyond purely material factors, at least when couched in terms of the direct impact of hazardous working conditions and poverty. In such arguments, not only is poverty expressed in relative rather than absolute terms, but lay people's responses to their social contexts must also be taken into account. For, even the ability to avoid health risks, as emphasized by Link and Phelan, suggests that mediating factors intervene between material conditions and health outcomes. Not all of those living in poor circumstances, for example, suffer poor health. In Link and Phelan's terms the processes that connect SES and the risks to health are 'dynamic'. The interplay of 'agency' and 'structure' becomes apparent here, as studies begin to explore the actions people take to protect their health, albeit under material conditions which exert powerful influences over them.

One of the most cited series of studies of health inequalities, drawn on by Link and Phelan, which raises wider questions about such health dynamics is the Whitehall project on heart disease among UK civil servants (Marmot et al. 1978, 1991). In the two studies concerned, Marmot and his colleagues have been following groups of civil servants over time, and documenting their health outcomes. These *prospective* studies have now been carried out over a 25-year period. Women as well as men were included in the Whitehall II Study. The respondents in the studies come from a variety of civil service employment that constitutes a hierarchy of different grades, ranging from office support and clerical grades at the bottom to the highest administrative grades at the top. The studies have shown that 'position in the hierarchy shows a strong correlation with mortality risk', with younger men in the lowest grades, in particular, having a 'four times higher mortality rate' from heart disease than men at the top of the hierarchy (Marmot 1999: 11).

As Marmot points out, all of these men are office-based workers, and at the time of the original studies were in relatively stable jobs and living in an affluent part of an affluent country. Even those in the lowest grades could not be regarded as living in highly deprived areas or in poverty. Yet their health patterns are clearly linked to their position in the occupational hierarchy. It could be, of course, that health itself has a 'selection' effect, such that those with better health move up the employment ladder over time, and those with poorer health move down. If the time period is long enough to observe the movement of a substantial number of individuals, this could help to explain the observed inequalities. Marmot notes, though, as others have done (e.g. Blane, Smith and Bartley 1993) that the effect of such 'health selection' appears to be small, and does not account adequately for the observed gradients found in the data. In addition, in the Whitehall studies, individual risk behaviours (smoking, alcohol consumption) appear to play only a small part in explaining the differences in heart disease between groups of civil servants. Less than a third of the social gradient could be accounted for in this way (Marmot 2004: 44). Even when the main risk factors are taken into account, significant differences in mortality are still found. The problem remains that while material, selection and behavioural factors alone cannot account for such health patterning, it is difficult to say what does. For Marmot (2004) steep gradients in the social hierarchy and problems concerning social status are what matter – the higher one's status, and the more control exercised over one's life, the lower the health risks.

It is here that the second perspective, that based on ideas concerning social cohesion and psycho-social stress, comes into play. If the materialist explanation derives its theoretical impetus from Marxian ideas of economic determinants, this second perspective is more 'Durkheimian' in character. Following Durkheim's work on suicide, an argument can be constructed which places as much emphasis on social relationships, social networks and social support as on material deprivation in influencing health outcomes. Here, the focus of attention is not so much on the issues of poverty and material hardship, but on inequalities in status and stress produced by a lack of social cohesion. Whilst deprivation may lie behind a lack of social cohesion, the emphasis on social networks and relationships brings culture and human agency more clearly into the frame.

Perhaps the best-known example of work produced from this perspective in recent years is that of Richard Wilkinson (1996, 2004). Wilkinson's research has received particular attention in the UK, as it refocuses analysis on the relationship between income inequalities and health, an analysis which, as has been argued, is more in line with US research on SES. Wilkinson's approach has been to challenge the prevailing approach to poverty and deprivation, whatever measure of social position is used. His main argument is that differences in health between social groups have persisted long after living standards have risen beyond the point where 'satisfying basic needs' is no longer a pressing issue for the vast majority of the population (Wilkinson 1996: 13). In so far as social and economic structures continue to exert their influence on people's health, it is through an understanding of issues such as insecurity in work and housing, social and community development, subjective quality of life, and 'above all . . . understanding the psycho-social effects of hierarchy and social position' that a more adequate explanatory framework can be constructed (p. 14).

For Wilkinson the position is quite clear. In societies where there is relative equality in income distribution, health inequalities are less marked. Where incomes are highly unequal, then similarly sharp health gradients can be expected. By adopting a comparative international perspective, Wilkinson attempts to show that differences in income *between* developed countries do not correlate well with differences in health status. It is *within* such countries that the relationship between social circumstances and health becomes more apparent. Beyond a certain 'threshold standard of living' (p. 75), further increases in per capita income do not make much difference. The USA, for example, has higher per capita income than the UK, but does not have a higher life expectancy or lower infant mortality. In short, 'what affects health is no longer the differences in absolute material standards, but social position within societies' (p. 75). In societies such as Sweden, where the income gradient is relatively flat, then health inequalities are less in evidence, though they do still exist. In countries such as the UK and the USA, the latter especially, differences are more marked, in both income levels and health gradients. Wilkinson agues that data on infant mortality and early adult mortality show that in Sweden, where narrower income differences benefit the whole population, including the poor, 'narrowing health inequalities give rise to faster improvements in national mortality rates' (p. 109). In other words, flatter income gradients not only help those at the bottom of society, but provide a healthier psycho-social environment for everyone (though see the opposing views on income differences of Judge et al. 1998, Lynch et al. 2001 and Gravelle et al. 2002).

The link between material and social factors in the Wilkinson argument lies in the notion of social cohesion. For Wilkinson, highly unequal societies with steep gradients in income produce societies which are 'dominated by status, prejudice and social exclusion', whereas more cohesive societies with 'high levels of social involvement' produce less marked social divisions and hence fewer health inequalities (pp. 171–2). Wilkinson goes on to discuss, more speculatively perhaps, the psychological and physiological pathways which translate or mediate the effects of highly unequal societies and their attendant stress levels, with their outcomes in terms of poorer health. Along with Marmot and others working in this vein, Wilkinson sees chronic stress as linked to changes in people's physical and psychological resilience, which in turn leads to increased risk of illness.

Alongside these different studies, a useful sociological framework for thinking through the possible connections between social structure, social cohesion and health has been provided by Berkman and her colleagues (Berkman et al. 2000). In this framework different groups of factors concerning both material and psycho-social pathways are brought together. The key mediating concept here is that of social networks, which are seen to act as buffers against deprivation, on the one hand, and to meet the practical and emotional needs that help to sustain health, on the other. These include, crucially, a sense of attachment. Rather than focusing on mortality and poor health outcomes, this approach considers the 'dynamic' involved in producing the social conditions that can help promote or sustain health in more general terms.

Berkman et al. outline a model, then, that deals with both 'upstream' and 'downstream' factors (pp. 846–7). In the first, 'upstream' part of the model, macro structural conditions are given prominence. Thus social cohesion, the presence or absence of racism or sexism, poverty and inequality, public policies and social change are all seen as important in helping to condition and shape social networks. Such networks then influence and interact with the situation 'downstream' in terms of the degree of social support, the presence or absence of close social ties and intimacy, and the adoption by individuals and groups of constraining or enabling positive health behaviours. Finally, the operation of social networks have an impact on health through psychological mechanisms (such as self-esteem and well-being) and physiological pathways such as immune responses and 'cardiopulmonary fitness' (p. 847). Rather than seeing lay people as passive victims of circumstance, this approach directs attention to the interaction between different levels of experience, including active social processes, such as social support and the cultural circumstances surrounding the adoption of health-related behaviours. These, in turn, interact with bodily processes.

Berkman et al.'s framework can thus help to explain the different findings presented by US sociologists such as Link and Phelan, and the research on health inequalities by UK workers such as Marmot and Wilkinson, by showing how they relate to different 'upstream' and 'downstream' aspects of health. In this way the debate has been moved forward from that offered by earlier approaches, such as the one presented in the Black Report, in which material and structural determinants of health were seen as determining health outcomes in a somewhat linear fashion. In a period of relative affluence, where the health of the population of developed countries has improved, an overemphasis on deprivation and poverty seems to be misplaced, though material hardship remains significant for a minority of the population. Whilst deprivation is clearly of continuing importance, the degree of inequality is just as relevant, if not more so, and this is the focus of more recent research. For a recent exchange of views and argument concerning the relative importance of material and psycho-social factors, see Lynch et al. (2000) and Marmot and Wilkinson (2001).

It must also be remembered that health inequalities in developed countries pale into insignificance compared with the health problems of many people in the 'second' and 'third' worlds, where average life expectancy and high infant mortality rates remain critical. There is also a danger, especially with the more complex models discussed here, that so many factors come into the picture that the thread of a cogent argument about the social determinants of health gets lost. The development of a life-course perspective on the social patterning of health, to which the chapter now turns, may offer a way forward in this regard.

Health and the Lifecourse

It should be clear by now that one of the conundrums that characterize the literature on the social patterning of health is how the observed patterns found in data on populations can be meaningfully related to specific groups and individuals. The 'dynamic' pathways approach discussed above is one way of thinking through these issues. This allows different factors to be related to each other, and crucial mediating processes such as social support and social networks (part of what is sometimes referred to as 'social capital') to be given due weight. Equally important, however, is the attempt to recognize that health risks rarely appear without having developed over a long period of time – so-called latency. Much of the illness burden today concerns conditions such as heart disease and cancer, that unfold with the ageing process. One way of dealing with this issue is to adopt a lifecourse perspective that sets out to show the ways in which health develops across time, both at the individual level and at the societal level. A lifecourse approach examines the interaction of biography and history, and therefore the processes that drive health of the kind outlined in the previous section, both positively and negatively. In particular, it can help develop a better understanding of why poorer groups may experience persistent health problems.

The ageing process, broadly conceived, is an important way in which to enter this particular aspect of the debate. The ageing of humans from birth onwards involves two interlinked sets of processes. The first of these comprises the biological, psychological and social development of individuals. The second concerns the experience of birth, maturation, old age and death as a member of a particular generation, living in a particular society, at a given period of history (Riley et al. 1988: 247). This temporal dimension of human development, involving the intersection of biographical time and historical time, has particular implications for the study of the patterning of health. Much of the data presented in studies such as the Black Report, discussed above, have a strongly 'cross-sectional' character to them – a 'snapshot' approach. That is, the data refer to events that have occurred in one place and at one point in time – for example, deaths among adult men or women in 1991–3 in England and Wales. Such epidemiological data are often collected with a number of purposes in mind, and this restricts what sociological interpretations may be placed on them. Routine statistics are rarely collected to answer specific research questions, and therefore explanations of the observed patterns have to be imported into the analysis after the event. Even major prospective research, such as that exemplified by the Whitehall studies, begins with individuals in their adult years. Whilst this kind of research can provide an important picture of health outcomes from the point at which the study begins, they cannot, of necessity, tell us much directly about the 'dynamics' that may have influenced the individuals before they were contacted.

In recent years a different, lifecourse perspective has been developed by epidemiologists and medical sociologists to try to overcome this serious limitation. Much of the debate in the UK has resulted from the pioneering work of David Barker (1998). Barker's work was originally concerned with heart disease in men born in two English counties. Through an examination of these men's health records, which provided details of their birth weight and early growth (they were born in the 1930s), he showed that death from heart disease later in life was more common in those who had been small at birth and at one year of age. This line of argument led to the idea of 'biological programming', such that the conditions *in utero* and in the period after birth had a strong determining effect on later life. More recent data from international studies – for example, of men born in Sweden 1915–19 (Leon et al. 1998) – have also shown the impact of foetal growth on adult heart disease.

In medical circles, the Barker hypothesis has proved to be particularly attractive. For some in medicine and public health, the renewed attention to individual biological development has been welcome, in contrast to the complexities and arguments that have surrounded more sociological explanations of health patterning. The Barker hypothesis has also held political attraction for those who regard interventions in later life as largely unwarranted. The repeated emphasis on the importance of changing individual risk factors, and calls for ever greater social regulation of health behaviours such as banning smoking, restricting alcohol consumption or advocating healthy diets, are often resisted in political circles. If health is strongly determined at birth, then a more measured, not to say relaxed, view might be taken about lifestyles and material circumstances in later life. 'Informed choice' by individuals becomes the guiding principle of health policy. Moreover, biological influences across the lifecourse appear to reassert the need for medical rather than social management of health risks.

However, the situation from a sociological viewpoint is somewhat more challenging. As Wadsworth (1997, 1999) has shown, the evidence for biological programming of health needs to be interpreted with caution. Wadsworth provides an illustrative example in the case of respiratory illness, specifically chronic obstructive airways disease (COAD – now usually referred to as chronic obstructive pulmonary disease, COPD), which includes chronic bronchitis and emphysema (Wadsworth 1997: 861). Despite considerable early research on work-based conditions and atmospheric pollution, and actions to improve both, mortality from COAD was not significantly reduced. Later research by epidemiologists, including Barker, showed that those developing the disease in adult life had poor respiratory function in their early years, and carried this with them into adult life. In addition, 'low birth weight, an indicator of poor growth before birth, was associated with a significantly higher increased risk of COAD and poor respiratory function in adult life' (Wadsworth 1997: 861).

Wadsworth argues that despite the importance of these early life factors, it is not clear whether such vulnerability – 'programmed in' at birth, so to speak – alone determines the onset of COAD, or whether other 'triggers' are necessary, and what part ageing plays in increasing risk. In fact, evidence regarding this condition and others shows the importance of interactions between early vulnerability and later life exposure. From this viewpoint, social processes throughout the lifecourse may be just as important as early influences in producing the observed outcome or pattern, and may drive underlying biological factors. To use the terms set out above, the development of such disorders can be seen to be the result of 'upstream' factors such as conditions at birth, inter-acting over time with more 'downstream' factors such as poor working conditions, lack of social support and risky health behaviours such as smoking. Unless these are carefully studied in tandem, the presumed determining influences of biological conditions at birth may be exaggerated.

By the same token, a sociological view would not, in any event, regard low birth weight or conditions in the first weeks and months of life as purely biological in character. The nutrition of mothers, the presence or absence of risky health behaviours during pregnancy, and other factors that can produce low birth weight are partly social in character and are open to sociological investigation. They are likely to be worse in poor social circumstances, and to be reproduced in many different ways across the life-course. But they are also open to intervention. 'Sure Start' pro-grammes in the UK (see <www.surestart.gov.uk>) and 'Head Start' in the USA (<www.acf.dhhs.gov/programs/hsb>) have attempted to put in place programmes to help poorer mothers and their children, both to prevent ill health (for example, through cessation of smoking) and to improve parenting skills and provide educational opportunities. These social interventions aim to confer both social and biological benefits on young children in particular, and thus to break the cycle that produces poor health across generations. Such programmes may also be attractive to politicians, who, though reluctant to pursue egalitarian policies and radical income redistribution – that is, to create a 'flatter' income gradi-ent, as advocated by Wilkinson – wish none the less to tackle particular aspects of social deprivation, especially child poverty (that is, 'relative poverty' applied to children's home circumstances). Maintaining income inequalities, perhaps even encouraging them as part of a vigorous market economy, are partially reconciled with anti-poverty and redistributionist policies enacted through such measures – at least in the eyes of some governmental agencies.

Whatever the outcome of such policies, attention to lifecourse dynamics and health patterning is now part of the sociological research agenda, stressing both the role of early development *and* the influences of conditions in adult and later life. In recent work, the issue of the interaction of biological and social factors has also been linked more closely to the study of the ageing process itself. Bury and Wadsworth (2003), for example, have examined the 'parameters' which biological development may set for health in later life. It is clear that essential aspects of the development of human bodies and their organs, including such issues as height, must occur within 'windows of opportunity', which, if missed, cannot be altered. The growth in height, for example, comes to an end in the late teenage years. Bury and Wadsworth accept that, in this sense, 'biological capital' is set in the early years of life. But to argue that this determines outcomes in later life, is, again, to neglect key features of experience and circumstance, even among older people. The adoption of healthy lifestyles in later life can confer real and lasting benefits on such individuals.

The point to be stressed here is that social contexts play a key role in the development and use of the amount of 'health capital' available from early life. As the lifecourse unfolds, and people grow older, social capital is likely to play an increasingly significant role, until, towards the end of life, biological determinants exert their influence once more. The interaction of biological factors with social processes across the lifecourse, through mechanisms such as social mobility, educational achievement, and membership of supportive social networks, can produce a variety of different outcomes. These processes may occur over considerable periods of time and reach into later life and old age.

Risks to health may similarly be shaped over long time periods, and be driven by both biological and social processes. Bury and Wadsworth consider the example of obesity in late middle age in relation to health problems acquired in early life. Analysis of data from a national study of health and development (the 1946 birth cohort study) shows that those who come from poor backgrounds (in both biological and social senses) *and* who are obese have a significantly greater risk of high blood pressure in later life than those who are not obese. Chapter 4 discusses this issue further in the context of health and the body. It is clear, however, that both social and biological risks to health are driven by social factors. Biological components of 'health capital' at birth and sub-sequently (here, raised blood pressure) are emergent properties, as contexts shape both behaviour and its outcome. And the health risk of obesity, paradoxical though it may seem, is increasingly associated with social conditions – that is, with deprivation. Poorer groups suffer more from obesity than those who are better off. Bury and Wadsworth argue that as a result 'for individuals, social and biological adversity may interact and accumulate from childhood to produce current and/or future risk to health' (p. 113). These interactions help to explain why some poorer groups carry reduced health capital with them into adult life and continue to experience increased health risks as time unfolds. By the same token, such interactions also help us understand how mediating factors that confer health protection – better education, or improved employment (itself dependent in part on structural processes) – can offset early adversity.

In a similar vein, Vagero and Illsley (1995) argue that in considering lifecourse influences it would be as easy to speak of 'social programming' as of 'biological programming' (Vagero and Illsley 1995: 231), and perhaps as equally misleading. If such an over-socialized perspective were to be adopted, then the effects of early social development, upbringing, educational experience, entry into work, and living conditions and lifestyle could all be seen as determining health in later life. Indeed, the more 'materialistic' approach to health patterning, as we have seen, comes close to arguing this case. However, Vagero and Illsley state, in contrast to both the Black Report and the Barker thesis, that 'biological and social influences are not mutually exclusive' (p. 232). A lifecourse perspective suggests that 'health development and social development are inevitably interconnected' (p. 232). Indeed, biological markers can be used as social indicators, and vice versa. Low birth weight and infant mortality have both been used in this way. Most importantly, social actions to offset health risks, whether by individuals or societies, can bring about significant effects. Whilst some degree of social inequality and thus health inequality may be inevitable features of modern society, this is quite different from arguing that nothing can or should be done to reduce their severity.

Part of the reason for adopting a lifecourse approach, when viewed from a sociological perspective, is thus to offer a critical perspective on over-stated claims about both early 'programming' and socio-economic determinants. Assessing the relative contribution of biological and social factors can then come to the fore in research studies. Clearly, biological damage to the individual, especially *in utero*, will set particularly tight limits for future development, but such problems may themselves be the result of social processes surrounding pregnancy. A lifecourse approach to the social patterning of health can also be adopted in different societies, taking into account the specific historical circumstances that obtain with respect to early life and later health risks. Clearly, being born in the USA or the UK in the 1980s or 1990s is very different from being born in India or sub-Saharan Africa in the same periods. But it is important that a sociological perspective directs attention to positive processes as well as serious problems, whatever the national socio-economic context. A lifecourse perspective can explore those factors that protect health or help to overcome adversity and promote health improvements. This holds out the prospect of a more positive and dynamic view of health development, and a reduction in the repetition of the fact that poorer groups have poorer health – a finding that is widely accepted and does not need to be constantly reiterated. Suggestions for positive improvements for health in the fields of economic and social policy need careful evaluation in their own right (Mackenbach and Bakker 2003), and should be set against lay experience of health inequalities in everyday settings (Blaxter 1993). Blaxter shows that preoccupation with inequalities may be less in evidence among lay people in everyday life, in comparison with experts, especially where health is seen to have improved from one generation to the next. For all of these reasons it is likely and necessary that the sociology of health will continue to explore health across the lifecourse.

Ethnicity and Health

Despite the gains in understanding that a lifecourse approach to health offers, it has tended to be applied to historical data on particular groups of national populations. This, despite its attractions and in contrast to more cross-sectional data, has its own limitations. Retrospective analyses, whether of the more biologically oriented kind provided by Barker or the more sociologically informed developed by Wadsworth, find themselves limited to particular historical groupings – for example, those born in England in the 1930s or 1940s. Significant social changes and contemporary issues may be neglected as a result of such a focus. Epidemiological research, in turn, has been criticized for its preoccupation with male mortality – an issue that will be dealt with in more detail in the next chapter on gender, sex and health. In each of these regards the rapidly changing social structure of developed countries such as the UK and the USA, needs to be recognized. The development of a multi-ethnic society is perhaps one of the most obvious cases in point. Whilst sociological interest in ethnicity has a long history, research on health and ethnicity in the UK, in particular, is now having to make up for lost ground. Though studies of immigration have been available for many years, until the 1991 Census it was not possible to collect routine data on different ethnic groups in the UK, though current research efforts are beginning to overcome this gap in the record. In the USA, where 'race and health' has been an established field of enquiry, groups such as South Asians and Hispanics are currently being accorded greater recognition.

The categorization of individuals and groups is always fraught with difficulty. This is particularly true with a term such as 'ethnicity' (and its problematic relationship to 'race'), where religion, language, appearance and place of origin can be variously important to its definition. As Smaje (1996) has pointed out, sociological divisions need to satisfy two broad needs: to explain a key area of experience in terms of identity, and to deal with the structuring of people's access to 'a variety of social resources' (p. 140). Such principles can be applied to many different conceptualizations, including social class, gender, age and national or regional allegiances. In the case of ethnicity, Smaje argues for a view that avoids 'objectivist' or 'essentialist' definitions, on the one hand, and 'postmodern' views, on the other, where boundaries and identity tend to be 'obliterated'. Instead, he argues for a conceptualization of ethnicity that captures the complexities of social life, including biological and cultural differences but also material disadvantages and the 'racism faced by many people from minority ethnic populations' (p. 166).

Yet, despite the need for care in conceptualizing ethnicity, Smaje recognizes the value of epidemiological and social research on the patterning of health by ethnic status, even when it is not theoretically informed. Despite the 'objectivism' of the term, Smaje quotes Marmot sympathetically: 'The vagueness of the term 'ethnic' . . . does not invalidate this area of study. If two groups, however defined, have different rates of disease, productive aetiological [causal] explanations may follow' (Marmot 1989; quoted by Smaje 1996: 152). Much of the empirical evidence on ethnicity and health, in countries such as the UK and the USA, has been gathered and analysed following this kind of general approach.

In the UK, for example, Whitehead (1992) in an update of the Black Report, notes that much of the work on ethnicity and health relied on information based on the country of birth as shown on death certificates (p. 258). She then provides a list of disorders, which compares the mortality rates of specific ethnic groups with rates for England and Wales as a whole. Liver cancer, for example, is comparatively high for Caribbeans, Africans and people from the 'Indian subcontinent', and hypertension is 'strikingly high' for immigrants from the Caribbean and Africa. Subsequent analysis, this time linking data from the 1991 Census (as mentioned, the first in the UK allowed to record ethnic origin) to death records, showed that 'overall mortality is low among Caribbean men

(SMR 89), but high for men in all other migrant groups' – that is, relative to the rate for all men aged 20–64 (Drever and Whitehead 1997: 111). These authors recognize that groupings such as these are not homogeneous, and they point out, for example, that class and age can have a major effect on the figures. Much of the excess mortality for those in social classes IV and V born in the Indian subcontinent is due to very high death rates among those aged 45–64. Younger men in those social classes have rates comparable to those for all men in England and Wales. It is also worth noting that in this later report, excess mortality among those from Scottish, Irish and Welsh backgrounds is reported.

It is clear that social class, material disadvantage and ethnicity interact in complex ways to produce health outcomes. Andrews and Jewson (1993), for example, point to data which show the 'remarkable pattern of diversity and change . . . that represents a challenge to many orthodox explanations for inequalities' (p. 138). In particular, they show that infant mortality rates do not follow an entirely predictable pattern. While rates are high for infants born into Pakistani and Caribbean families, they are low for Bangladeshis. Yet, the latter group is one of the most materially deprived communities in Britain. Explanations for these different patterns are to be found, according to Andrews and Jewson, 'in the context of configurations of social relationships' (p. 142) – that is, in the complex mix of 'health capital' and 'social capital' that influence health outcomes. The presence of supportive social networks, for example, may offset, at least to some degree, the impact of material hardship. In a sample of some 8,063 white and minority ethnic populations living in England and Wales, Nazroo (1997a, 1997b) found a similarly complex set of results concerning both physical and mental health. Some minority ethnic groups had higher levels of poor health, compared with whites, while others did not. Social class alone could not explain all of the variations; racism remains important (Karlsen and Nazroo 2002).

In the USA, David Williams (2000), among others, has examined the 'dynamics' of class and race in American life, and the way in which racism and residential segregation 'have created adverse living conditions that are pathogenic for minority populations' (p. 21). Like the British researchers whose work was discussed above, Williams analyses data for leading causes of death taken from large-scale data sets, in this case the US National Center for Health Statistics, comparing the experience of minority populations with that of the majority white population. The picture that emerges is a complex one. While the black population has higher levels in almost all of the ten leading causes of death, especially heart disease, stroke, diabetes and HIV/AIDS, Hispanic and American Indian populations have comparable or lower rates for a number of leading causes, including heart disease and cancer, but higher rates for diabetes and cirrhosis of the liver. Asian and Pacific Islander populations have lower rates for all the leading causes of death, though Williams maintains that as the length of stay in the USA increases, 'the health status of immigrants deteriorates' (p. 22).

These data reinforce the view that *within* group variations are as important as *between* group variations, and that there is considerable heterogeneity in minority ethnic populations. For example, the presence of significantly lower rates of respiratory disease but much higher rates of HIV/AIDS among Hispanics suggests that different pathways protecting or elevating risk need to be explored. The presence of protective factors (here, for example, in producing low respiratory disease) may have implications outside the Hispanic population. At the same time, Williams shows that the black population has an 'overall death rate that is 1.6 times higher than that of the white population' (p. 22). Higher rates are found in eight out of the ten leading causes of death. Despite an overall reduction in mortality for all groups, the relative position of blacks as compared with whites has worsened over the last 45 years. Much of the observed difference is accounted for by differences in socioeconomic status (SES), and although those from higher SES groups within the black population have better health than those from lower SES groups, 'at every level of income, for both men and women, African Americans have lower levels of life expectancy than their similarly situated white counterparts' (p. 24).

Official statistics cannot easily reveal the pathways that have led to this complex situation. Williams is surely right, in the case of poor health among African Americans, to point to the long-term effects of racism, restricting access to educational and employment opportunities, and also to residential segregation. Such segregation is also reflected in the fact that '[t]wo-thirds of African American students and three-fourths of Hispanic students attend schools where more than half the students are black or Latino'. In itself this may not be a negative factor, except that it is associated with 'concentrated poverty' (p. 28). Exposure to racism can also have a direct effect on health, not just via socio-economic position, for example, but through restricting access to medical care, and the subjective stress of discrimination. However, those factors that help protect some minority ethnic populations and some groups within them is less clear. The role of positive biological capital and social capital, whether cultural, in terms of values which help to promote educational achievement and positive health behaviours, or in the form of supportive networks, is in need of closer analysis. The mediating role of family and kinship structures – itself a controversial aspect of debates about the different life chances of minority ethnic groups – is likely to be an important explanatory dimension.

In a review of arguments and evidence regarding health and ethnicity in the UK and the USA, Smaje (2000) reiterates the point that medical sociology is concerned to take a critical view of how 'race' and 'ethnicity' are defined and used, while at the same time being open to the real effects that social position and social processes such as racism can have on people's lives. Each country has a complex picture of migration and settlement, reflecting differing patterns of colonial and other events, including in the US, of course, the long-term effects of earlier patterns of slavery and social exclusion. Overall, Smaje argues that while health indicators in the USA and the UK show that ethnic minorities have worse health than whites, the picture is far from straightforward. In some instances the situation is clear, in others not. Deaths from homicide in the USA, for example, are seven times greater for African-American males than for white males. In the UK, while heart disease rates are higher for some minority ethnic groups, cancer rates in general are lower (Smaje 2000: 118). The importance of studying the patterning of ethnicity and health lies in the fact that it tells us not only a great deal about the experience of differences in power and resources between 'racialized groups', to use Smaje's phrase, but also about the possible mediating effects of social networks and cultures that can either increase or protect against health risks. Such an approach can provide an important contribution to the sociological study of health patterning in general.

Health and Place

In the previous section, the point was made that the effects of racism and/or economic deprivation can be traced, in part at least, to *place of residence*. Smaje (2000: 121) argues that the effects of place on health are difficult to disentangle. In the case of minority ethnic populations, residential concentrations of a particular group may increase health risks, especially in low-quality urban areas. Even here, though, some communities may be protected by developing and defending supportive networks which promote health-related behaviours – for example, in the area of diet. Access to health services may also, of course, be influenced by the place in which people live. Whilst most developed societies have achieved a much better provision of health services for their populations over the last 30 to 40 years, geographical and social inequalities in access and quality of care remain (Dixon et al. 2003). The importance of studying place and health lies in the fact that it can help to move the sociological focus up from the individual level (or from aggregates of individuals, as is often the case in epidemiological research) to a more collective or social level of analysis. A brief consideration of place in the patterning of health can therefore usefully conclude the present chapter.

The analysis of patterning of health by geographical location is not new. Variations in health between rural and urban settings, and between regions (for example, in comparisons between the north and south of England), have long been studied. Indeed, they formed an important part of the Black Report, and have been documented in many reports since (e.g. Doran et al. 2004). Recent sociological interest in place and health, however, has stemmed from a desire to distinguish between 'social composition' and 'social context' in geographical locations. According to Joshi et al. (2000: 144), the former deals with the 'aggregated characteristics of individuals', and the latter with characteristics of an area 'independent of its individual inhabitants'. We return again here to the difference between health as an attribute of individuals and health as a relation between people. In emphasizing the latter, the study of place and community-level dynamics offers the promise of bringing together agency and structure in understanding health pathways more fully. It is worth quoting, in this respect, the various factors that Joshi et al. identify in this more contextual form of analysis:

> Context could include features of the physical environment, such as climate or pollution, and features of the local economy, such as the housing stock or the structure of employment. It could also include the provision of services such as shops, transport and schools, as well as the quality of the healthcare available. Finally, there are features of the social fabric which may make a place more or less 'healthy', such as the level of crime or community cohesion. (p. 144)

Here, too, we can identify both structural issues and the more Durkheimian approach to social cohesion discussed earlier. In fact, the analysis provided by these authors suggests that both the effects of geographical area *and* the characteristics of individuals are important in explaining observed patterns of health. They suggest that policy must be able to combine initiatives that target individuals and the communities in which they live. The effects of living in a particular place, however, do not appear to be easily separated from the health characteristics of individuals. If an individual lives with others who smoke, then it is more likely that the individual will do the same.

In a review of recent work on the topic, Macintyre et al. (2002) have argued that, despite this difficulty, studies have shown the independent impact of place on health. Studies from the USA in particular have demonstrated that when the effects of individual-level health behaviours are accounted for, the effect of living in 'poverty areas' was still significant (p. 128). In general, however, they agree that a more 'differentiated picture' suggests that interactions between individuals and place are crucial to the social patterning of health. In order to bring greater conceptual clarity to these processes, Macintyre et al. suggest that the nature of the importance and meaning of 'place' in sociological enquiry needs to be specified more clearly. They propose that a hierarchy of 'universal human needs' be adopted, in order to evaluate the nature of the health effects of specific geographical locales. At the top of the hierarchy are such issues as clean water and air and adequate supplies of good-quality food. In the middle are education, work and health care resources, and at the bottom are religion, group activity or provision for cultural and physical recreation (p. 133). Of course, it is moot where different judgements might place items in this hierarchy, but the point of this approach is to suggest that specific hypotheses could be formulated, to examine particular pathways that lead to particular health outcomes. Macintyre et al. give the example of heart disease, which they say could lead to the investigation of individual risk factors in relation to environmental hazards and to cultural norms governing health behaviours in a given locality. In this way both 'material and non-material' factors can be investigated as they influence the social patterning of health. The more that health risks are seen as a feature of community characteristics, the more social and political action to provide security, safety and a healthy environment enters the debate.

Concluding Remark

The sociological and epidemiological study of health patterning has shown that many factors can determine health. Using measures of mortality or morbidity (including disability), an inverse relationship between social position and health status has been consistently found in many studies and in many countries. Much depends on the degree of inequality in income and material conditions that prevails. More disadvantaged groups have poorer health than those in more privileged settings, though within-group difference can be significant. Not everyone living in deprived settings has poor health, and the mediating role of social networks and social support is of importance. More recently, debates concerning health and the lifecourse have examined the interactions between biological and social processes that affect health over time. The complex pathways that determine health are revealed particularly in recent studies of ethnicity and health. Finally, the examination of place and health allows sociological enquiry to develop a more contextualized form of analysis, stressing the role that community and cultural-level factors can play in health. In all of these forms of enquiry the dynamics that produce health outcomes are the result of human agency and actions, as well as of the effects of social structure.

Note: Since 2001 the UK Office for National Statistics has introduced the National Statistics Socio-economic Classification, in an attempt to reflect changes in occupational structure, work practices and the changing position of men and women in the work force.

3

Gender, Sex and Health

In the last chapter an attempt was made to portray the 'dynamics' of social influences on health across the lifecourse. In this chapter, the focus is more specific: namely, on the influence of gender. At the same time, the complexity of what is involved in linking gender and health will be no less apparent than it was in dealing with other social divisions. There are a number of reasons for this, not least in deciding what is meant by 'gender'. Sociologists and feminists alike have relied on a clear distinction between biological 'sex' and sociological 'gender'. As Annandale and Hunt (2000: 24) comment, many feminists are loath to abandon this distinction, in order to continue to highlight 'preventable differences' in health between men and women. If sex and gender are treated as synonyms, or as so diverse in their meanings as to make little sense as separate categories, then those health-related issues that arise from the distinctive patterns of women's and men's social roles and positions may be lost.

As we saw in the last chapter, however, the patterning of health is in important respects biologically driven, and sex is one dimension on which this can be observed. Women cannot fall prey to cancer of the testes, and men cannot develop ovarian cancer. Apart from health disorders and diseases built into women's and men's different biological make-up (especially those related to their reproductive systems), some diseases also seem to be a fixed part of sex differences that unfold with the ageing process. Arthritis, for example, is more common in women than in men, and Parkinson's disease is more common in men than in women – both major causes of disability in later life. Reasons for this are largely unknown, but it is unlikely that the observed differences can be easily accounted for with respect to gender roles or social circumstances. How such disorders are responded to by the wider society, and how they are treated in a given health care system, are, of course, different matters, and may well be influenced by such processes.

In addition to these considerations, health, disease and illness cover many different kinds of phenomena, from minor ailments to life-threatening disorders. Links between them and whole sections of a given population (such as women or men) are likely to be mediated by many factors. Women and men may share experiences in terms of their gender, but these are likely to be cut across by class, age and ethnicity (Annandale and Hunt 2000: 6). Whilst gender is a central feature of identity, its ubiquity weakens its sociological explanatory power. If half of the population is being referred to in the analysis, as it often is in discussions of gender, it stands to reason that many kinds of within-group differences are likely to be present, whether recognized or not. For example, social class differences among men and women can be highly significant. Highly paid or wealthy women, for example, may have little in common with their poorer sisters in terms of material circumstances and life chances, despite some similarities in experience.

A final introductory point should be noted. Much contemporary sociological writing on gender and health struggles with reconciling ideological arguments about women's subordinate position in society (including their outright 'oppression') with social change. Many feminists remain wedded to the idea of contemporary society being patriarchal in character, and to the idea of patriarchy as a key concept in explaining gender differences in health. Yet patriarchy has at least two meanings: literally, as a system of inheritance through the male line (favouring the oldest son), and more generally, as a system of male dominance and rule (which, in turn, may have implications for health). Patriarchy in the first sense is particularly characteristic of traditional and early modern societies, whilst the latter meaning could be applied to any society where men hold sway in key areas of public and private life. Most feminist analysis appears to invoke the latter meaning, though it is rare to find the term clearly defined. In any event, as many feminists themselves have argued, gender relations have changed considerably in recent years, and this needs to be taken into account in any analysis. Gender roles have been affected, amongst other processes, by women's increasing involvement in the labour force, greater financial independence and the rise in the numbers of lone mothers (Arber and Cooper 1999: 62). Both health and gender, and the social conditions to which they relate, have a dynamic and complex character.

It is important, therefore, in this area as in others, that sociological analysis does not overreach itself. It cannot answer all of the puzzles that health and its possible determinants throw up. Some health-related issues constitute an important terrain for examining the influence of gender inequalities compared with sex differences, whilst others are more equivocal. In addition, whilst women's health has been central to analyses of gender and health, a *comparative* perspective suggests that both women's and men's health need to be seen in relation to each other. Though it is understandable that women's health (particularly as related to childbirth) has received particular attention from feminist sociologists, more systematic comparisons that would allow clear conclusions about gender influences to be drawn are needed – what Annandale and Hunt (2000) have recently referred to as an 'inclusive' research agenda (p. 11). Moreover, analyses need to focus on gender at different stages of the life-course, so that variations in experience by age can be examined (Arber and Cooper 1999: 62; Arber and Cooper 2000: 123).

In order to examine these questions more fully, the chapter proceeds by three steps. First, it reviews some of the evidence on differences in health experience that can be attributed to gender, in terms of both roles and social structural position – that is, on gender inequalities. This section reviews evidence from studies of life-threatening disorders, before considering the experience of those of a more common and chronic kind, including mental health problems. The section then goes on to review lifecourse influences, including the impact of age on gender and health. Second, the chapter considers gender differences in the expression of illness and in help-seeking behaviour, examining in particular evidence for the argument that women report more illness. Third, the chapter concludes with a note on the issue of the meaning of illness in a period of rapid change in gender relations.

Gender Inequalities in Health

Mortality and survival of women and men

As will become clear in the course of the following discussion, the patterning of health by gender needs to be seen in pluralistic terms: in patterns rather than a singular pattern. Some differences in health between men and women are marked, while others are not, and some are mediated by social factors such as income, class or ethnicity, while others are more specific to gender relations as such. To repeat the point made above, correlating two halves of the total population with the wide range of phenomena that constitute human health is unlikely to produce a satisfactory picture, on logical grounds alone.

Even so, some parts of the picture are clearer than others. Thus, in developed societies today men, overall, have higher mortality rates than women (at all ages) and lower life expectancy. In 1901 males had an average life expectancy at birth of around 45 years, and women 49 years. By the year 2000 these figures had risen to 75 and 80 years respectively (ONS 2002: 120). It needs to be remembered that life expectancy figures are expressed as an average, and that such averages were low in the past largely because of high death rates in infancy and early adult life. Annandale (1998: 127) has also noted that the pattern of 'female advantage' – that is, lower mortality and higher life expectancy – is a relatively recent feature of modern society, and is not found in many developing countries, where female mortality can be higher than that of males.

The reasons for 'male disadvantage' – high mortality and low life expectancy compared with females – in developed countries are many and various. The main cause of death, which helps explain the observed difference, is coronary heart disease (CHD), and illustrates the complex mixture of biological (sex) and social (gender-related) factors that influence health and illness. In a review of data relating to the USA (though with implications for similar patterns in other developed countries), Waldron (2001: 40) argues that CHD accounts for about one-third of the difference in mortality between women and men. Probably the most important factor at work here is the rate of smoking, which, with few exceptions (for example, among some groups of teenagers), is higher among men than among women. Even among non-smokers, men have higher mortality from CHD than women. Biological differences play an important part here, influenced, in turn, by social and cultural processes. Waldron notes that in terms of weight gain, men have a tendency to increase abdominal fat, with implications for the functioning of the heart, while women put on weight in the lower part of the body (Waldron 2001: 42).

In addition to heart disease, some common forms of cancer have also contributed to the relatively poor survival of men, compared with women. Lung cancer is an obvious case in point, and is largely related, again, to differential smoking rates. Indeed, Waldron notes that if the effects of smoking are excluded from the analysis, 'sex differences in cancer are very small' (p. 42). She goes on to note, however, that occupational exposures (for example, to coal dust and asbestos) have had an impact on male cancer mortality in the past, and that obvious sex differences in reproductive anatomy and hormonal effects all contribute to the resulting 'gendered' patterning. Waldron summarizes the situation by saying that differences in cancer mortality are influenced by 'multiple behavioural, anatomical, and physiological differences between the sexes' (p. 42). Recent findings on the genetic contribution to conditions such as breast cancer may be added to this list.

Despite this relatively clear picture of male disadvantage and female advantage in mortality, and thus in survival, a number of caveats need to be entered. Two are of particular note. The first is that the data reviewed by Waldron refer to the situation as it obtained in the USA in the 1970s, 1980s and early 1990s. Whilst some of these data are still relevant, considerable changes are under way in the economy and culture of countries such as the USA and the UK, with respect to health risks, such that caution needs to be exercised in accepting the picture as fixed. Annandale (1998) provides a discussion of some of the social processes that are altering the distinct experiences of women and men, and gender relations themselves. These point to a possible process of 'convergence', involving, for example, a faster decline in male mortality compared to that for women, though Annandale is keen to emphasize the unfinished nature of this possible trend (p. 130).

Perhaps the most important of these changes concerns working life. Most developed countries in recent years have gone through a major restructuring of their economies, such that heavy industry (with its attendant risks to physical health) employs far fewer men than it used to. Between 1971 and 1991 the number of people (overwhelmingly men) in the UK working in the industrial sector fell from just over 9 million to under 5.5 million. Coal mining, for example, has all but disappeared in many parts of Britain, including areas such as South Wales, where it was once a major employer. By contrast, service industry employment in Britain (involving more women as well as men) rose in the same period from over 12.5 million to just under 18 million (Law 1994: 91). In 2001 only one in ten female and one in five male employees worked in manufacturing (ONS 2002: 76). The largest private employer in the UK today is the supermarket chain Tesco, with about 200,000 employees, the majority of whom are women.

The dramatic reduction in male employment in heavy industry and the increase in women's participation in the economy (albeit with nearly a half of working women in part-time employment) have, arguably, led to a degree of 'equalizing' in working life, especially among the young. However, a recent analysis of social class differences *amongst* women and *amongst* men (which illustrates the persistence of marked gradients in health status favouring the better-off in both genders) has shown that occupation still has a strong influence on male mortality. For females, differences in the social standing of the household is shown to be more important than their occupational status as individuals (Sacker et al. 2000). Thus the changing dynamic of the economy and its impact on domestic life have produced a number of varying effects with respect to health.

Part of what is at issue here are changes in women's and men's risk behaviours. Up to the 1980s men consistently smoked more cigarettes than women, but for the last 20 years the decline in smoking has been somewhat greater for men than for women (though both are smoking less, overall) to the point where their rates are approaching 'convergence' (Annandale 1998: 134). Similarly, and as Waldron (2001) points out in her discussion, men in the UK (especially young men) have had higher rates of traffic accidents than women. A male propensity to engage in 'risky behaviours' is clearly demonstrated here, in driving at greater speeds and with less care. Annandale points out that stricter laws and the emergence of influential social norms governing drink driving, together with the introduction of compulsory seat belts, has helped to reduce male deaths. Reduction in female deaths from the same cause, though present, has been less marked. The development of 'ladette' behaviour among young women, in which risk behaviours once thought to be the province only of young men are adopted, may be adding to this process of convergence. Here, changes in culture and gender relations can be seen to play a part in reducing 'female advantage' and 'male disadvantage' in turn. It is somewhat ironic, however, that the equalization of health risks should in part be the result of women adopting some of the more deleterious (and at times anti-social) 'male' forms of behaviour.

The second caveat that needs to be noted, with respect to mortality and survival differences between women and men, is that the data on these differences may reflect biases shaped by 'gendered' assumptions. The two main causes of death, discussed above, CHD and cancer, both demonstrate this difficulty. It is sometimes forgotten, by female as well as male commentators, that heart disease is the most common cause of death for women after cancer. The preoccupation with reducing male mortality from CHD (the rates of which have been high, though there have been signs of definite and sustained improvement in recent years) has obscured its presence among women. As Doyal (1995) has noted, there has been little medical research on non-reproductive conditions of women, and few studies have explored differences between the sexes in conditions such as CHD. Sociological research on women's health, and on heart disease, may have had a similar effect, giving tacit support to a research and policy agenda in which the female experience of conditions such as CHD are downplayed (Lockyer and Bury 2002). The image of the 'type A' male, which conjured up the stressed businessman as being particularly at risk, was at the expense of recognizing the importance of CHD among women and among men from lower socio-economic backgrounds (Bartley 1985; Marmot 1998).

The same point holds true for lung cancer, another major cause of death in women as well as men. While male rates of the disease remain higher than female rates, there has been considerable improvement in recent years among men. Citing data from Scotland, Annandale makes the point that there has been a steady (though small) decrease in the incidence of lung cancer among men for every five years since the mid-1980s, but for women there has been a noticeable increase. In England and Wales, 'male deaths from lung cancer nearly halved between 1971 and 1992, while female rates increased by a sixth' (Annandale 1998: 135). Death rates from lung cancer amongst women are now close to those from breast cancer, though the latter has had much more medical and public attention than the former. This illustrates that choosing the point of comparison can make a great deal of difference to what and how particular disorders come into view. If high male mortality is taken as the starting point, the significance of women's mortality from 'male' diseases, such as CHD and lung cancer, may be neglected. And if women's 'advantage' in survival is the focus, then improvements in the same life-threatening conditions among men may be missed. This multifaceted and dynamic character of health and gender under conditions of change (what Waldron 2000: 155 calls the production of 'diverse patterns') is even more evident when we turn to morbidity – that is, to the occurrence and experience of illness rather than survival or death.

Gender and illness experience

Alongside assumptions connected with the higher rates of mortality among men have been equally powerful ones concerning higher morbidity (illness, disability) rates among women. The main assumption has been that despite women's 'advantage' in life expectancy and low mortality, women tend to experience more non-life-threatening illnesses than men. These include chronic conditions and disorders that are sometimes referred to (especially by medical authorities) as 'trivial' complaints. Behind this assumption lies the idea that while men have led more hazardous and risky lives, women have experienced more health problems as the result of oppressive gender roles. This picture of illness and its causes has led to the oft-repeated, but as we shall see, questionable saying that summarizes gender health differences: 'men die but women get sick.' Of course, in a period of relatively low mortality (the majority of deaths in developed countries today occur in old age) the patterning of health and illness in terms of morbidity takes on greater salience, for *both* women and men.

One of the reasons for arguing that 'women get sick' is the widely held belief that gender roles produce threats to women's long-term health as the result of 'patriarchy'. In particular, it is argued that the relative lack of control and the inequalities experienced by women in many spheres of life (economic, public and domestic) underlie much of the gendered patterning of illness. Low status and income can produce 'entrenched inequalities' in health (Annandale and Hunt 2000: 1).

Relative powerlessness may be accompanied by psychological and physical harm, together with the indirect effects of an increase in health risk behaviours, such as poor diet or higher levels of smoking. Changes in structural and cultural conditions linked to such risks could also help explain some of the reduction in 'female advantage' in mortality discussed in the previous section.

Despite arguments along these lines, and their relevance to thinking about the differential experience of women and men in society, comparisons of morbidity experiences have recently undergone substantial revision as empirical data have thrown new light on the subject. It is now more widely recognized that non-life-threatening illnesses and disability are too broad a set of categories to fit into neat conceptual or theoretical boxes. Whilst some forms of illness do show strong gender patterning, others do not. Moreover, as we have seen, health and illness are constantly changing phenomena, both at the experiential level and in terms of their understanding by researchers and medical practitioners. Just one factor alone – a greater recognition, for example, of heart disease among women – can alter the situation, by bringing a whole group of women into focus and hopefully enhancing the care they receive.

Within the limits set by this ever-changing pattern of illness, studies have now begun to provide evidence for a more fine-grained picture of the different experiences by gender. In a major review of findings from two large surveys of health and illness in everyday settings, Macintyre et al. (1996), for example, have shown that in many cases of minor ill health, expected differences between women and men do not follow the anticipated direction. The data here are taken from the 'Twenty-07' study of young and middle-age women and men in Glasgow, and the Health and Lifestyle Survey (HALS), a national study of health among adults in Britain, conducted in the mid-1980s. From these surveys, Macintyre et al. derived a number of measures of health, including self-assessed health, a checklist of 18 symptoms experienced in the last month, and a list of chronic and episodic conditions.

As far as self-assessed health is concerned, although younger respondents in the 'Twenty-07' study did show a difference between genders when asked to rate their health as either 'fair' or 'poor', with women reporting a higher level of poor health compared with men, this did not hold for other age groups or with other measures of general health. Macintyre et al. comment: 'there were no significant gender differences in the percentages reporting any longstanding nor any limiting longstanding health at any age for either study' (Macintyre et al. 1996: 619).

When the list of symptoms was examined in more detail, a mixed picture emerged. For symptoms that might be thought of as having a strong psycho-social component, such as 'worrying', 'nerves', 'always tired' and 'headaches', the most consistent excess was apparent among women. For other symptoms – for example, 'back trouble', 'colds or flu', and 'persistent cough' – no pattern was evident. In the case of two symptoms, 'palpitations' and 'trouble with ears', a male excess in the older group of the 'Twenty-07' study was found. A mixed situation also emerged from the chronic and episodic conditions. Apart from more arthritis among older female respondents in the surveys, no difference between women and men was found for conditions such as diabetes, hernia and high blood pressure (p. 620). Macintyre et al. conclude that 'the direction and magnitude of sex differences in health vary according to the particular symptom or condition in question, and according to the phase of the life cycle' (p. 621). They note, however, that 'the more psychological manifestations of distress' were consistently found more frequently among women of all ages.

Evidence from other studies has reinforced this mixed picture of gender patterning in health. Annandale, for example, has shown, in an analysis of official morbidity data from general practice in England and Wales, that 'women suffer far more frequently from mental disorders, specifically from anxiety states and depression, osteoarthritis, migraine, obesity and iron deficiency anaemia', but that in a range of other conditions there is no consistent pattern, and in some cases (for example, heart disease symptoms) rates are higher for men (Annandale 1998: 145). Annandale comments that 'we need to avoid drawing any sweeping conclusions that women are sicker than men' (p. 146). Even so, it is clear here, too, that mental health problems in particular show a consistently higher rate for women compared with men, especially the 'affective' or 'neurotic' disorders such as anxiety and depression.

In an analysis of current trends in psychiatric morbidity, Double (2002) cites figures from a government community-based survey of mental health in the UK, showing that 'the proportion of men and women with a neurotic disorder in a given week was found to be 12.3% and 19.5% respectively' (Double 2002: 901). Double also notes that throughout the 1990s the annual number of prescriptions for antidepressants in England rose from around 8 million in 1991 to around 22 million in 2000. It should be noted that the figure of 22 million prescriptions is for only one class of drugs, anti-depressants, and that these are taken more by women than by men. The interpretation of such figures, for either symptoms or drugs consumed, however, needs again to be treated with caution. In many forms of illness, but especially mental illness, factors influencing recognition and reaction to symptoms are many and various. For example, though rates of anxiety appear to be higher in women, heavy use of alcohol, considerably higher among men, may mask their experience of anxiety. And the rise in consumption of anti-depressants may mean that women (and men) are taking such drugs at a lower level of symptoms, rather than that there is an increase in clinically depressive illness.

Age, gender and health outcomes

One way to explore the various factors that might be responsible for this complex pattern of health and illness among women and men is to take into account social circumstances and roles across the lifecourse. Annandale, drawing on evidence from a number of studies, argues, for example, that paid work outside the home may be beneficial for women's health in general, as it contributes to an accumulation of roles and expands opportunities for social support and improved self-esteem, but that much depends on age and related circumstances. From this viewpoint, younger full-time 'housewives', with no roles outside the home, are likely to have the worst health of all (Annandale 1998: 148). This is confirmed by other studies (Bartley et al. 1999: 105). At the same time, whilst for women over 40 years of age with children, paid work seems to confer health benefits, for younger women with children, multiple roles can produce considerable 'role strain' – having to deal with the demands of the 'outside world' during the day and the demands of home life in the evenings and at weekends. Arber and Thomas (2001: 99) refer to this as the 'double shift' that many such women have to perform. As Lorber, reviewing research in an American context puts it, 'juggling work and family responsibility may be more stressful for women than for men' (Lorber 2000: 62). Bartley et al. comment from their study that 'full time working mothers had a significantly increased risk for poor health compared with mothers with part-time or no paid employment' (Bartley et al. 1999: 105).

Most importantly, the emphasis on lifecourse influences directs attention to the interplay between historical circumstances and the experience of different age groups. Arber and Thomas (2001) note, as discussed earlier, the significant changes in gender roles that occurred during the last century, especially for women and men in advanced societies such as the USA and the UK. Increases in paid employment for women and the adoption of more 'home-oriented' roles among many men are, today, in marked contrast to even the recent past. As Abercrombie (2004: 32) points out, however, changes in roles does not mean equality. Moreover, particular historical periods produce different effects. For women today, for example, health in mid-life will have been influenced by the pattern of child bearing and child care which they experienced in the 1970s and 1980s. With the reduction in family size and an increase in the number of women with no children, the future for many women in developed countries, despite the inevitable strains of child rearing, will be significantly different from that of their mothers and grandmothers. Educational achievement also influences later position in the labour market, which in turn affects status and income throughout life. The links between different phases of the lifecourse within specific historical contexts are therefore at the centre of this approach, rather than age groups being treated in isolation (Arber and Thomas 2001: 101).

As we saw in the last chapter, in contemporary societies the health and circumstances of older women and men can be seen to reflect their differing experiences in childhood and in adult life. Older men have enjoyed full employment throughout their lives, and many will have served in the Second World War (Arber and Cooper 2000: 140). For women, the influence of marital status is particularly significant, with half over the age of 65 being widowed, compared with only 17 per cent of men. Income inequalities among older people have become marked in recent years, with a large divide opening up between those with occupational pensions and those relying on the state pension. Fully two-thirds of older women in Britain today are in the latter category. Even so, material circumstances do not map on to 'gendered' health variations in later life in any simple way. When self-assessed health is considered among older people, Arber and Cooper find only modest gender differences (with older women reporting slightly higher levels of health as 'less than good'), in contrast to disability levels, which are considerably higher among women. We have already noted the importance of arthritis in women (largely biological in its origins), and this helps explain much of this difference. However, Arber and Cooper's main point is to highlight the considerable 'within gender group' differences in health among older people, especially the long-standing influence of their social class backgrounds. Higher proportions of previously professional women and men rate their health as 'good', compared with those from a semi- or unskilled occupational background, indicating 'the resilience of social class during working life in influencing health into very old age' (Arber and Cooper 2000: 143).

Similar patterns of health across the lifecourse, and into old age, have been observed in the USA. Estes et al. (2000) have noted that the longer life expectancy of women is accompanied by a number of social and health outcomes. Like Arber and Cooper in the UK, Estes et al. note that half of those aged 65 years and over, and more than two-thirds of those aged 85 and over, are women. Stressing a 'political economy' approach to ageing and the lifecourse, Estes et al. argue that 'women's dependency on the state [for income and health care] grows with age and the loss of spouses and other means of economic and social support, just as health and functional status are declining' (Estes et al. 2000: 137). As in the UK, the economic and social position of women in later life can be particularly precarious, resulting from female patterns of 'employment and marital instability' across the lifecourse, relative to older men. But, unlike in the UK, where older people have a measure of health protection through the NHS, older women in the USA are, according to Estes et al., forced to rely on health and social care (through the Medicare and Medicaid systems) that are based on a privatized and 'sold for profit' basis, rather than in terms of health care as a right (p. 134). We should note, however, that in the UK, social and long-term nursing care is increasingly linked, in part at least, to the individual's ability to pay.

Estes et al. draw attention to another important feature of age and health in contemporary society: namely, that of ethnicity. Patterns of disadvantage resulting from the inequalities produced by social class and income are compounded by ethnic inequality. Whilst ethnic minorities comprise only 1 per cent of the British elderly population, reflecting the historical pattern of migration, stemming particularly from the 1960s, race has been central to the US analysis of later life over a much longer period. Minority groups are projected to comprise one-third of the elderly population in the USA in the next 50 years. Estes et al. argue that 'the 'color line' is the most important division of society' (2000: 137). Data on poverty and ill health in the USA show consistent patterns of disadvantage for older African-American and Latino populations. Estes et al. argue that 'older African Americans and older Latinos have two to three times the poverty rate of white elderly, and many do not have health insurance' (p. 137). Existing inequalities in health status between African-American and white elderly populations (with African Americans being less healthy and more disabled) are also likely to increase in future, partly as the result of increased rates of diabetes and hypertension (p. 137).

But in considering the links between age, gender and health outcomes, it is important to strike a cautionary note. However significant the inequalities are, whether the result of lifetime differences in occupation and income or the effects of different patterns of state provision – and the evidence clearly shows that they *are* significant – an overemphasis on poverty and dependency among older people can have unintended consequences. The *relative* differences in health experience and social and economic circumstances between women and men, and *among* women and men, by social class or ethnicity should not mask overall improvements in living standards and even health where they are evident. The presence of a social hierarchy (whether conceptualized in terms of patriarchy or not) does not mean that no positive changes have taken place during recent times.

As has been noted, there have been profound changes in working and domestic life, affecting millions of women and men. Some of these have had measurable benefits for health. The reduction in family size, for example, has reduced women's exposure to the hazards of multiple pregnancies, a common experience even 50 years ago. Moreover, though there is considerable debate about evidence which suggests that the health of older people is improving (possibly as the result of younger age groups bringing a 'healthier profile' into old age as they retire), an overemphasis on poor health, as well as on dependency and poverty, can reinforce negative stereotypes of the elderly (Bury 1995, 2000a). For many, if not the majority of elderly people, the possibilities of a relatively more healthy and more comfortable old age – even among minority ethnic groups – is a real prospect, as recent data from American researchers are beginning to show (Manton and Gu 2001). The difficulties associated with growing older should not detract from gains that have been made, including those resulting from medical procedures such as hip replacement and treatment for cataracts, which have brought untold relief from pain and disability to many elderly people. The fears of medicalizing old age need to be balanced against the real need which older people have for effective medical interventions. An overemphasis on poverty and dependency can also detract from the active steps older women and men take, and have always taken, to protect their health and enjoy their later years.

Illness Behaviour and Help Seeking

The last point, concerning the active steps taken to protect health, brings us to questions of help-seeking behaviour and the use of health services. Even a short review of the patterning of health by gender, such as this one, would not be complete without considering how gender roles and social circumstances influence the expression of illness and decisions to seek professional help. If sociological analysis focuses entirely on the social determinants of health, as if they work in a linear fashion, it will miss the complexities of social action which mediate symptoms and their expression. Not all health problems are acted upon, and not all help-seeking behaviour is related to objective signs and symptoms of illness.

To return to the example of coronary heart disease (CHD) for a moment, the review by Lockyer and Bury (2002) summarizes a number of studies which show that the cultural imagery surrounding CHD, as a disease of stress among affluent men in developed countries, misses two important factors. The first, as mentioned before, is that among men those from poorer backgrounds have higher rates than those from professional groups. This is in line with the general discussion of 'health patterning' discussed above and in chapter 2. Second, and more importantly for current purposes, the assumption that CHD is essentially a male disease may have led to women being less likely to receive diagnostic tests, less likely to receive treatments such as surgery, and more likely to be referred for specialist help only later in their illness (Lockyer and Bury 2002: 433). The lower rates of CHD among women may have added to the widespread perception that heart disease is not significant for them. Women and their doctors may both have underestimated the importance of the disease. The significance of CHD as a major cause of death and disability among women is therefore strongly mediated by social influences and culturally produced perceptions, and is open to remedy by a more 'gender-sensitive' approach to diagnosis and referral for treatment. Stereotypes and imagery surrounding illnesses can have real effects, especially when they influence what is thought to be 'normal' for women or for men. Even sociological research on heart disease which explores lay perceptions (Davison et al. 1991, 1992) has concentrated almost exclusively on beliefs about the disease amongst men.

More generally, the 'presentation' of a wide range of health disorders for professional help may also be strongly influenced by gender roles. Despite (perhaps because of) the possibility of 'under-recognition' of life-threatening disorders such as CHD among women, sociological analysis of illness and help-seeking behaviour has suggested that women are more likely than men to report non-fatal and chronic illnesses, and more likely to seek medical help for them. Just as morbidity (illness) rates have appeared to show that women are more likely to be sick than men, it has often been argued that women also use health services more than men. There are a number of reasons why this might be so.

The first concerns the nature of illness in relation to 'gendered' patterns of emotional expression and attention to the body. If men are thought to be reluctant to admit to illness as the result of 'macho' attitudes, or pressures not to take time off work, then women can be portrayed as having a more 'accepting' attitude towards illness. In addition, caring (or 'nurturant') roles towards children and other dependents (including sick husbands, partners or parents) can lead women to be more sensitive towards health and illness issues, and to be more likely to be in regular contact with health services. As Lorber (2000) puts it, 'women are not more fragile physically than men, just more self-protective of their health' (p. 43). It has also been argued that the 'sick role' is more compatible with women's domestic roles, in that women are not under the same pressure as men to remain at the 'economic front', and are able, as a result, to take time off from their normal roles and 'be sick'. Finally, it may simply be the case that women live more stressful lives, and are therefore more likely to be ill and require medical help (Popay and Groves 2000: 69–70), though, as has already been seen, the evidence for women being 'more sick' is equivocal.

Yet, as Popay and Groves note, there are, in any event, substantial reasons to be sceptical about arguments showing that gender roles lead to greater help-seeking behaviour among women. Whilst it may be the case that 'macho' views of the emotions and the body play some part in explaining the reactions of men to symptoms, the pressure to maintain work roles is increasingly affecting younger women as well as men. Similarly, while many women remain responsible for the health and well-being of their children and others, this does not necessarily mean that their roles make sickness or the sick role more acceptable or more available. The opposite may be the case, where role strain and the 'double shift' make it *less* likely that women will be able to 'go sick'.

In a further study of gender and health behaviour by Macintyre et al. (1999), no simple pattern of 'over-reporting' of health was found which might give credence to the view that it is women's roles that lead them to report more illness than men. This study examined responses by a sample of women and men in the 'Twenty-07' study in Glasgow to questions and prompts about their help seeking in response to specific conditions or symptoms. In fact, replies to an initial 'global' question about their health showed that there were no significant differences between women and men in terms of their propensity to report illness. After further questioning, men were, interestingly, found to be more likely to seek help for their symptoms. There was also no evidence in this study that women were likely to report higher levels of mental health or 'trivial' complaints. Whilst caution needs to be exercised in interpreting these findings, if only because they are of what people said about their health and reporting behaviour, and not of 'objective' measures of either, they suggest, as before, that no simple 'gendered patterning' of health behaviour can be presumed. Much depends on the kind of health problem under discussion and the context in which action is taken to deal with it.

Having said this, there is evidence to suggest that gender can play a role in *some* forms of health service use, and that women in particular continue to have more frequent contact with health services than men. In a major study of health service use and help-seeking behaviour, Rogers et al. (1999) reported on empirical findings from a study of primary care (community-based health services and general practice) in the north-west of England. The Pathways to Care study sought to unravel the threads that tie people into different forms of help seeking and service use. It found that, in particular, people's perceptions of symptoms had a bearing on how they reacted to difficulties with their health. Those in more affluent areas often blamed a single environmental cause, whereas those from poorer backgrounds had to contend with multiple sources of deprivation, such as poor housing and unemployment. Managing illness and seeking help were inevitably set against the specific contexts in which they occurred, together with the presumptions held about the causes of illness and the value of seeking professional help in the face of them (Rogers et al. 1999: 82–3).

In responding to the onset of symptoms in oneself or in someone else, knowledge of symptoms and the practice of self-care influences the decision to visit a doctor, and this is likely to be mediated by social networks. Women in the Pathways to Care study often remained at the centre of evaluating alternative actions and their likely benefits, and in decision making about help seeking. Rogers et al. state that 'women are more likely to facilitate access to professional care and exercise greater control over network members' health behaviour than men, have larger more multi-faceted networks and report more supportive relationships' (p. 112). Such control may not be immediate with respect to a particular illness episode, but may be the result of long-term knowledge about illness and health action, which is then 'stored up' for use as and when needed (p. 122). Women were seen to regulate their own use of services in order to ensure that appropriate treatment was obtained for their children and other dependents. Finally, there were suggestions of a gendered pattern of health seeking in the study, such that 'women acted as proxies for men who did not wish to articulate their health needs, and where contact with formal health services would not otherwise have occurred' (p. 122). Although women may not be 'more sick' than men, their roles as carers bring them into contact with health services more frequently, and this may help explain the appearance of an 'over-use' of health services in comparison with men. Such 'over-use' is more apparent than real, once the focus shifts from the health needs of the individual to the role women play in decision making and help seeking within familial and social networks.

Gender, the Meaning of Illness and Social Change

It is perhaps inevitable that any discussion of gender and health will produce a complex picture. As argued at the beginning of the chapter, gender represents a huge division of the population, if treated in a simple male/female fashion. Each gender group is cut across by differences in age, class ethnicity, and a host of other variables. Some of these map on to a male/female gender division in a straightforward way, though many do not. Even the same illness may be experienced under very different circumstances, producing a different trajectory and a different outcome. Moreover, health is such a large area of human experience, ranging from the most insignificant to the most threatening of symptoms, that it is hardly surprising that much sociological discussion in this area stresses the complexities at work. Whilst some forms of 'minor' mental health problems may affect women more than men, and whilst some aspects of service use stem from gendered patterns of caring, many of the differences between women and men are less than clear-cut, and others are simply differences stemming from biological differences.

A number of points can be derived from this complex picture. First and foremost is what can be called the 'general susceptibility/specific cause' problem. By this is meant that many of the observations of gender differences – that is, those health experiences that can be attributed to the structure of male domination in society – constitute a general susceptibility towards illness, expressed in terms of broad measures of morbidity, including chronic illnesses. The long-term stresses of gendered roles are held to produce many of the differences in health found among men and women. But, once many of the non-life-threatening disorders are broken down into specific symptoms and signs, and examined more closely, much of the presumed difference disappears, as the evidence from studies such as those by Macintyre and others discussed above has shown.

In addition, considerable changes in the economy in developed countries, with attendant changes in the domestic sphere (smaller family size, postponement of age of marriage, high divorce rates), undermine any simplistic picture of unchanging gender relations. Whilst Popay and Groves (2000: 85) rightly argue that women's economic inequality, lack of power and responsibilities for child care 'remain salient', changes in gender relations are of significance and may be resulting in changes in illness susceptibility. Differences that have been attributable to gender relations may be lessening, partly as the result of the relative improvement in men's health. An improvement in mortality among men in conditions such as heart disease and cancer *may* meet women coming the other way, as women are drawn further into the economic sphere and engage in lifestyles and health behaviours once thought to put men at particular risk.

Having said this, it is important not to overemphasize the possibilities of a worsening in women's health in this connection. Bartley et al. (1999: 104) report that self-assessed health (itself a good predictor of health in later life, and even of mortality) improved over the nine-year period of their study, 1984–93. They comment that there was a sharp reduction in poor assessed health, and that there is 'evidence that general levels of health [among women] are improving'. This, they argue, is partly a result of rising employment among women and an increase in household living standards.

Indeed, such is the rate of change in the economic and social position of women and men in society that some feminists have contended that a process of the 'feminization of the lifecourse' is under way. In part, this is a function of changes at the population level. As Arber and Ginn have pointed out, the existing gender differential in survival is such that in early old age there are 25 per cent more women than men, and that among the 'very old' (over the age of 85) there are three times more women than men (Arber and Ginn 1991: 9). When these population characteristics are considered alongside changes in the economy, and in marriage patterns and family size, the social dominance of men and of male values at all ages seems less than secure. In early adult life and in the middle years, the picture of the male worker and the female home-builder, in particular, is undergoing substantial revision. The health needs, values and outlook of an increasingly feminized society are likely to be at the centre of analysis, whether feminist-inspired or not. Though recent improvements in male survival may be altering the demographic profile of lifecourse 'feminization' (Arber and Ginn 2004), more general social and economic processes (including notably a rise in the proportion of female employment) continue to exert their influence.

If, as Popay and Groves (2000: 67) argue, the existing 'narrative' surrounding gender and health ('men die early but women get sick') is no longer adequate to address the 'diverse landscape of subjective experiences' that constitute health, where does this leave the argument that patriarchy is at the root of the differences that *are* observed? If women's health advantage in the past (lower mortality and higher life expectancy) emerged 'alongside a remarkable improvement in their social status and economic circumstances' (Annandale 1998: 128), can the fact that women's income remains lower than men's (having 'roughly half as much money as men', p. 137) have a continuing, significant and deleterious influence on their health, in comparison with men in the future? This chapter has argued that despite some increases in the rates for selected life-threatening conditions among women (such as lung cancer in some areas of the UK and the USA), it seems unlikely that this will happen, especially if absolute living standards continue to rise, for both women and men. As Annandale herself discusses at some length, a complex picture of 'convergence' between women's and men's general susceptibility to poor health (within a general context of better survival for both sexes and lower levels of some forms of illness) is the most likely trend.

Concluding Remark

It seems clear that as the earlier narratives surrounding the gendered pattern of health and illness are becoming less relevant, so the meanings attached to illness, by both women and men, are also changing. An analysis which relies on a poorly specified notion of 'patriarchy' will fail to capture the many paradoxes and cross-currents that go to make up the gendered patterning of health, and the influences on women's and men's responses to the problems they face. Moreover, as a more nuanced picture of gender and health emerges, the meanings attached to gender relations themselves, as well as to health, will need to be researched more carefully. The sociological literature on changing sexual relations and on the nature of intimacy, for example, suggests that women and men are actively engaged in fashioning the contexts in which they live. They do not simply respond to them as 'external' determinants. Recent commentators on the changing nature of gender relations, such as Connell (2002), Abercrombie (2004) and others discussed above, have tried to capture some of these dynamics.

In this context it is of interest to note, finally, that the positive effects of sexuality and what Jamieson (1997) calls 'disclosing intimacy' (with their different shades of meaning across the lifecourse) on health and well-being are surprisingly absent from much of the current sociological discussion of gender and health. Yet, a range of research from the 1970s onwards has demonstrated that intimacy and social support have positive effects on health, especially mental health (Busfield 1996: 197–8). Abercrombie (2004: 26) notes, more generally, the value of research which gets behind public debate and the stereotypes of masculinity and femininity, stressing the differing patterns of living and loving.

The emphasis on social processes, such as low level of control, poor living standards and the oppressive character of social structures (whether strongly patriarchal or otherwise), in much of the sociological analysis of gender and health leaves little room for these more positive aspects of gender relations. The 'gloom and doom' which characterizes much writing on the subject undermines an approach which could emphazise the 'agency' of women and men in fashioning their lives, within the constraints they face. Those factors that protect and enhance health should surely be as important to sociological analysis as those factors that appear to compromise it. As elsewhere in medical sociology, it is time, perhaps, to recover and develop such positive themes, and to integrate them into the new narratives of health and gender that are now emerging.

4

The Body, Health and Society

Introduction

The first three chapters of this book have dealt with different aspects of health and illness: their conceptualization, patterning and structuring by social divisions such as those of social class, ethnicity and gender. Even though it is often absent from view, in each case the body is involved in a variety of ways. Research on morbidity and mortality, is, in the last instance, about what happens to human bodies. Even in everyday talk, any conversation about health touches on matters to do with the body, if only as the site on which health and illness are 'inscribed'. When we talk of symptoms or signs of ill health (running a temperature or noticing a rash, for example), we are conscious of changes to the body. In most everyday settings, and for most of the time, the body, like health, is a given, 'taken-for-granted' reality which sustains our lives and the pursuit of valued goals, whether listening to a favourite piece of music, engaging in sport or working. It is often the case that only when such activities are disrupted by the onset of illness that we become conscious of our bodies. It is true, of course, that much of our waking hours are spent attending to our bodily requirements, in terms of what clothes to wear, what food to eat and many other physical needs besides. We also monitor the performance of our bodies on a continual basis – checking on how energetic or tired we feel, for example, or whether to take in food or drink. But, if we were fully conscious of our bodies throughout our waking lives, social action would be almost impossible. The taken-for-granted character of the human body serves its own functions.

In recent years sociologists, especially those interested in health and illness, have argued that the body should have a more prominent and explicit part in sociological enquiry. This has gone hand in hand with attention to other aspects of human experience which appear to have been neglected in sociology, such as a greater recognition of the emotions in social life and in health (Bendelow and Williams 1998). The argument that the body should be 'brought back in' to sociology is, perhaps, a little wide of the mark, if only because it has never really been prominent in sociological enquiry, though this has been less so in the history of related disciplines such as anthropology (Bury 1997: 178–84). Nevertheless, more explicit attention to the body raises a number of important issues, to do with the linkages between the individual and society, and is thus worth attention in its own right. Although recent interest in the sociology of the body and health has largely been a feature of British medical sociology, a number of writers in North America have made a considerable contribution to the subject and will also be discussed in what follows.

The chapter organizes the topic of the body, health and society around four main themes. The first is the nature of the body as both a biological and a social entity. The chapter reiterates the argument that regarding health as a dynamic process entails seeing biological and social realities as interactive in producing health outcomes. Second, the chapter discusses the 'absent presence' of the body in sociology, to use Shilling's (1993/2003) phrase, and examines different approaches to the experience of illness when viewed in terms of the body, focusing particularly on the work of Frank. Third, the chapter focuses on disability and the body as a means of deepening the discussion, taking as its point of departure the definition of the disablement process, one of the most contested issues in sociology in recent years. Finally, the chapter concludes by reviewing some of the main criticisms of focusing on the body which have emerged in recent sociological discussions.

Biology, Sociology and the Body

In the last chapter it was argued that feminist sociologists had supported their arguments for greater attention to social divisions and inequalities between men and women by separating biological sex from socially organized gender roles. Distinguishing the biological and the social in this way was, for many such theorists, a 'conceptual breakthrough', to use Connell's phrase. The now familiar argument ran thus: 'Sex was the biological fact, the difference between male and female human animals. Gender was the social fact, the difference between masculine and feminine roles, or men's and women's personalities' (Connell 2002: 33). What appears to have made this distinction attractive was that it chimed in with widespread and popular sentiments concerning divisions between the mind and the body, nature and nurture. The body and nature were seen to be fixed, while the mind and nurture (including gender roles) were seen to be open to social intervention.

A view of the body as natural and fixed has also fuelled a related conception of the body as a machine (Connell 2000: 30). This, like the separation of mind and body, can be seen to be derived from ideas dating back to the French philosopher Descartes (1596–1650), who saw the body as obeying natural laws and put forward a view of the mind (or, in Descartes's language, the 'soul') as a separate entity; matter was of a different order from mind (so-called Cartesian dualism). At our death, Descartes argued, our bodies simply lose their vitality and decompose, but our souls depart and enter the immortal realm. In this way, the body could then safely become the focus of scientific enquiry and be regarded in materialistic or mechanistic terms. In the seventeenth and eighteenth centuries it was not uncommon for 'natural philosophers' to conceive of the body as a system of mechanics and hydraulics. The idea, for example, that the heart was a pump, and that blood circulated round the body, was discovered and propounded by the English physician Harvey, a contemporary of, and influence on, Descartes, in the years following 1616 (Porter 1997: 213). The view that the body is a machine, and that the mind and the body inhabit separate realms, has frequently been derided by sociologists as reductionist and 'essentialist', even though, as has been noted, distinctions between nature and nurture, or the body and society, have characterized much contemporary and 'radical' thought.

Despite the fact that there are many grounds on which mechanistic conceptualizations of the body can be opposed, their persistence is in many respects understandable. Though, as this chapter goes on to discuss, treating people and patients as machines can seem to invalidate important aspects of experience, or be used by health care practitioners as an excuse not to recognize and respond to the subjective nature of illness, a materialistic and mechanistic view of the body has proved to be a powerful resource for improving knowledge about the body, and a means of significantly increasing the quality of life of millions of people. Many examples could be given. The case of heart disease alone could suffice, considering the enormous and growing success of programmes of heart bypass and heart valve replacement operations that exist throughout the world today. Those working in such programmes often refer to the operations involved with phrases such as 'doing pumps', a term which could not be more mechanical in tone. If other examples such as hip replacement (largely the result of developments in bioengineering), eye surgery, transplantation, effective pharmaceutical treatments (based on biochemistry) and more are added, it seems perverse, to say the least, to convey the idea, as some sociologists do, that Western thought about the body since Descartes has been fatally flawed. Whilst it is true that the necessary process of involving individuals in their treatment, and helping them to recover in the short and long term, involves much more than treating the body as a machine, crucial parts of the process are inevitably based on mechanistic ideas.

Nevertheless, there are clear limits to the use of mechanistic metaphors, and to working with mind and body as separate spheres. In the first place, as Connell notes in his discussion of gender, such an approach often assumes that bodily characteristics are fixed or invariable, even when they are not. For example, the physical characteristics of men and women change considerably over the life-course, from a starting point in infancy, where many such differences between the sexes are quite small, to larger differences during child and early adult development (Connell 2002: 29). Just as important, perhaps, is the fact that differences *within* groups are often as significant as differences *between* them. Although, as children grow older, boys will tend on average to be taller than girls, there are in adult life 'many individual women taller than many individual men' (p. 30). Connell also notes that differences in bodily organs such as the brain, thought by some biologists and psychologists to embody fixed male and female characteristics, have been found to be much smaller than has often been supposed.

A more fruitful starting point for considering the body and health, therefore, would seem to be one of viewing the body and the social environment as interactive. The dynamic nature of health and human development offers a number of possible lines of thought following this approach. Chapter 2 suggested that, when viewed as a process unfolding over time, the body itself is shaped and altered by social processes, and in turn interacts with the environment to produce particular effects (Bury and Wadsworth 2003). The question of height, mentioned in the earlier discussion, has received considerable attention in social and epidemiological research, especially its links with the social patterning of health. As noted, in human development the growth of the body occurs within certain biological limits. Height gain can only take place within a set time, and around the age of 20 it stops. The developmental opportunities for bodily growth cannot finally be circumvented, though the way they proceed can have varying outcomes. Thus, children who are larger at birth (itself partly a product of social circumstances, as smaller, low birth weight babies tend to be concentrated in poorer groups) and thrive well, with good nutrition, will do better physically and be somewhat taller than those who lack these advantages. Moreover, across generations and in periods of economic growth, individuals will tend to be taller on average than their parents (Kuh and Wadsworth 1989). Thus, from the outset, it is clear that biological and social factors influence the way the body grows and develops.

In adult life, social influences can be seen to play a greater role in the body and in health, but again, the processes are dynamic, interacting with the environment positively or negatively. In Bury and Wadsworth's discussion, the example of obesity and being overweight is considered, using data from a large study of individuals born in England in 1946 who have been followed periodically since that time (Wadsworth 1991). At the age of 43 the sample was examined to identify those who were obese or overweight, and the consequences of this for health – in this instance defined as having raised blood pressure. It was clear that those people from poorer backgrounds, in terms of both their physical characteristics at birth (such as their height at 2 years) and their social circumstances (such as father's social class), were more likely to be at risk for high blood pressure, but this was made worse if they were obese or overweight. The combination of high risk in childhood and obesity or being overweight in adult life had a significant effect. The percentage of the group that had a combination of the two had raised levels of blood pressure, and was significantly greater than those who were not at such dual risk.

In this example we can see how physical characteristics of the body and health risks are mutually reinforcing. Both have social correlates. Although being obese or overweight has independent effects on health, and can be seen in part at least to be the result of motivated action on the part of the individual, the condition is not randomly distributed in the population. As Bury and Wadsworth show, obesity is significantly higher among poorer groups. Indeed, Prentice and Jebb (1995) report that up to 50 per cent of women from manual social class backgrounds in the United States are clinically obese. Recent evidence from the UK shows that in 2001 over 20 per cent of adults were obese, with 30 per cent of women in 'routine occupations' and 16 per cent in 'professional occupations' being so classified (ONS 2004: 111). Substantially higher proportions in all social groups were designated as overweight. In this way the body can be seen as being shaped literally by social processes. In turn, such changes to the body influence physical functioning and health by producing (in this example) a greater risk of raised blood pressure and heart disease, together with disorders such as diabetes. An interactive view of body and society helps to identify the complex pathways that lead to such observable effects, as the life-course unfolds in particular cultures and at particular times.

In this context, the changing pattern of work and employment for adults, and its impact on the body in contemporary society, is particularly revealing of the effects of wider social structures, as well as behaviour, on health risks. As Freund et al. (2003) have pointed out, in the first half of the twentieth century employers in countries such as the USA and the UK followed 'Fordist' and 'Taylorist' principles, in planning the time and speed of production in order to increase productivity and efficiency. This meant that 'time and motion' studies were employed to regulate workers' activities, and thus their bodies, in the production process. 'Overload' and 'underload' often resulted (Freund et al. 2003: 99). Overload occurs where demands on the body are linked to such practices as piecework, and where the speed of work is too fast for the body's 'natural rhythms', leading to physical stress or exhaustion. Underload, by contrast, is where work is repetitive and boring. Whilst not all boring work need be stressful, much of it is, engendering the feeling that the body and mind are not being used in an optimum way. The combination of overload and underload in repetitive and physically stressful tasks is thus particularly damaging to health. Freund et al. review a number of studies examining the health correlates of such bodily 'wear and tear', including outcomes such as increased levels of heart attacks among workers involved in 'hectic monotonous work' (p. 100).

Although Freund et al. go on to make the point that many of the strict 'Taylorist' principles are no longer applied in most workplaces, the general outlook is still present in many forms of management. Today, in the USA, workers put in more than 49 hours a week, many of them now in white collar employment, which has expanded rapidly in recent years. Although global changes have increased the pressure on workers in Europe as well as in the USA, the latter country still has fewer rights to vacation time. Freund et al. state: 'The United States has no requirements for paid vacations, and the standard paid vacation (when employers offer one at all) in the United States is less than half as long as in Europe' (Freund et al. 2003: 101). This situation, together with more 'flexible' working patterns (often involving shift or 'rotation' hours), reduces the degree of control the worker has over work and the demands it places on the body. The issue of control over work has become the focus of a number of research projects, examining its impact on the body and health, especially in relation to disorders such as heart disease. Low levels of control over work have been found to be a significant risk for heart disease, as well as other disorders (Marmot 2003; Marmot 2004: 129). These are linked to changing employment patterns and inequalities in life experiences of the sort examined in Sennett's recent book on respect (Sennett 2003), in his discussion of the need to maintain self-esteem. Marmot's work points particularly to the bodily and health effects of low self-esteem, and the need to be able to balance the 'demands and rewards' of working life. Here, too, the contextual and interactional view of the body and the social structure is underlined, affecting health at crucial stages of the life-course.

The Sociology of the Body and the Experience of Illness

It is important to bear in mind the above discussion as the issue of the body in wider debates in sociology and medical sociology is now considered. A perspective which sees the body and society as dynamically interactive can help in interpreting the various lines of argument that have been put forward, as the examples of gender, height, obesity and work have already illustrated. Separating the biological from the social produces a one-sided account of the processes at work, however useful it might be for dealing with specific aspects of physical functioning, such as how the heart or a hip joint works. In this section the discussion moves from considering interactions of the body and society in the occurrence of health disorders to considering their place in the *experience* of health and illness.

A number of sociologists have argued that the body has taken on particular salience in a culture dominated by greater individualism and self-awareness, and in an economy which emphasizes consumerism and body maintenance (Giddens 1991; Shilling 1993/2003). Indeed, Shilling maintains that in such circumstances the line between the natural and the social becomes blurred, as the body is manipulated and altered by technical and social interventions. A range of instances can be cited. Assisted reproduction, for example, accounts for between 1 and 2 per cent of births in many developed countries today (in Denmark it is 5 per cent), a small but not insignificant proportion. Medical 'enhancements' such as breast implants are increasingly common (Conrad and Jacobson 2003). Both of these examples will be discussed in more detail in the final chapter, on the future of health. Clearly, such developments challenge earlier conceptions of how the body should be regarded and acted upon. Moreover, developments such as transplantation involving animal organs (so-called xenotransplantation) and manufactured products further significantly erode the idea of an integral or holistic 'natural' body. In addition, body images are now subject to considerable change, with dieting producing a desired slim shape for some, while over-eating and lack of exercise leads to obesity for others. Despite the health risks of obesity, it is currently being 'normalized' in cultural segments of countries such as the USA and the UK, as clothing and other accoutrements for oversized people are being produced, in what we may be tempted to call an expanding market.

Shilling argues that though many of these sociological preoccupations have taken on a new impetus, the body is not an entirely a new topic of analysis. Classical sociological theorists such as Marx, Durkheim and

Weber, he argues, all had important things to say about the body. These were usually implicit, however, and rarely focused on the body as a subject matter in its own right (Shilling 1993: 27–8). Following more recent sociological writings of Elias and Bourdieu, Shilling reiterates a line of argument that should now be familiar to the reader: namely, that the body can be seen as a form of 'physical capital' which is employed by individuals to achieve social goals, in conjunction with 'social capital' accumulated through education and other social processes. Shilling (2002) has aligned these concepts with a re-evaluation of Talcott Parsons's work on health and illness, and has emphasized the notion of health as a form of 'capacity' to be found in the Parsonian perspective on social life. Such an approach clearly echoes the above discussion of the dynamic involved in the body interacting with the social environment to produce health outcomes.

In this part of the discussion, however, the emphasis shifts to arguments that call for sociological attention to the experience of bodies and health. An emphasis on subjective experience leads Nettleton and Watson (1998) to call, for example, for a sociology of 'embodiment' rather than a sociology of the body. These authors argue that the idea of 'embodiment' reminds us that 'the self and the body are not separate and that experience is invariably, whether conscious or not, embodied' (Nettleton and Watson 1998: 11). In the experience of illness, the 'lifeworld' of the individual, comprising his or her biography and values, is confronted with bodily change and disruption. 'Biographical work' is needed to attempt to repair and restore a sense of secure self-identity (p. 12). Nettleton and Watson cite the late Irving Zola to the effect that the taken-for-granted character of embodiment, and especially the cultural barriers to speaking about the body, have hitherto created a ring of silence around the subject (p. 20). This private world of bodily experience, or 'embodiment', has been left largely unexamined by sociology, in comparison with many other areas of enquiry.

However, there are now such large literatures on both the sociology of the body and the experience of illness, in the UK and the USA at least, as to make calls for a more explicit focus on the topic somewhat redundant. Mention has already been made of Freund et al.'s summary of research on work and the body in the USA, and this is set within a wider consideration of health experience (Freund et al. 2003). Whilst it is true, as Nettleton and Watson (1998) note, that much sociological writing on the body has been overly theoretical in tone, an increasing number of empirical studies on experiential issues are emerging (their own collection being a case in point). In the rest of this section the discussion will focus on some of the key arguments in Arthur Frank's writings (1991, 1995), which have documented in detail his own personal experience of illness and, through contact with a variety of patient groups, that of others. Whilst falling short, perhaps, of a systematic research programme with a clear methodology, Frank's influential work illustrates many of the themes currently being explored in sociological studies of the body and illness, and can therefore stand as an exemplar.

In his earlier book, *At the Will of the Body* (1991) Frank describes his experience in early middle age of developing heart disease and then, as he was getting over this, discovering that he had testicular cancer. The first part of the book is a poignant account of the disruption and discontinuity that this sequence of events created for him. Frank had to come to terms with an altered body and simultaneously an altered life. The loss involved was not only that of physical functioning, but also of his younger self. Until the onset of his illness, Frank had been able to see his present as a continuous link with his past, but now he had to recognize that his past was over – 'like saying goodbye to a place I had lived in and loved' (Frank 1991: 39). He and his wife had to face the possibility of disruption to the future as well, with the normal expectations about life and survival being compromised. But Frank emphasizes that the sequence of events was not as orderly as his writing about them suggests. This 'disorderliness' he relates partly to the nature of specific illnesses as, in contrast to most cancers, where the fear of sudden death is absent, in heart disease it may be ever present, at least in the acute phase.

The 'differences and particularities' of illnesses and their expression in the body of individuals, Frank argues, are difficult for people dealing with the ill to manage. The employment by health professionals of categories, protocols and guidelines may help the practitioner, but may strike the patient as insensitive. It is the particularities of experience that give meaning to illness for the individual, but these are almost impossible for others to take on board. How each person in the care-receiving/care-giving relationship handles these tensions can play a large part in determining the experience. Care-givers in particular, Frank argues, are 'confronted not with an ordered sequence of illness experiences, but with a stew of panic, uncertainty, fear, denial and disorientation' (Frank 1991: 49), though he adds that even for the sufferer such words have little reality 'until filled with an ill person's own experience'. Current attempts to create 'managed care' and 'evidence-based' practice (to be discussed in the next chapter) can easily clash with patient experiences, however much such initiatives are designed to do the opposite. The heterogeneity of illness experience, including the anxiety and dependency it can create, sits uneasily alongside such rational procedures.

In such a situation, the individual patient is vulnerable to the reactions of others, especially those professionals giving immediate care. Frank states that when he was ill, 'I needed others more than I ever have, and I was also most vulnerable to them' (p. 70). The ethos of appearing to be positive before professionals carried its own costs, where recognition and acceptance of fear and pain would have been more reassuring. This was even more acute, as, when treatment for his cancer left Frank with additional problems such as the loss of his hair, the stigma of cancer was 'embodied' in the effects of chemotherapy. Though some of the professionals whom Frank encountered recognized these dimensions of his experience, many did not. He argues in the book that for medical staff, 'continuing suffering threatens them, so they deny it exists' (p. 101). Echoing the earlier work of the anthropologist Kleinman (1988), Frank argues that 'simply recognizing suffering for what it is, regardless of whether it can be treated, is care' (p. 101).

Despite this call for professionals to 'witness' patients' suffering, there is within *At the Will of the Body*, a more optimistic theme, which emerges at least when recovery or improvement occurs. This is taken up and developed in a further volume, *The Wounded Storyteller* (1995). Frank argues that a number of important changes have occurred in 'late modern' or 'postmodern' societies, which assign illness experience and the body increased relevance. One of the most critical of these is the transition from the predominance of acute life-threatening illnesses (especially the result of infections) to a situation where chronic illnesses and long life expectancy are more typical. Frank argues that, as a result, we now live in a 'Remission Society', where very large numbers of people, possibly the majority, are either suffering from illness or living with its aftermath. Many disorders and diseases which would have once killed the patient can now be managed through technical intervention and treatment, and this produces circumstances in which individuals and their families 'share the worries and daily triumphs of staying well' (Frank 1995: 8).

For Frank, such changes create a social context in which illness is experienced not so much as disruption but as part of 'life's map' or 'life's journey' (Frank 1995: 7). Hence the title of the book. Patients and lay people, Frank argues, are now reclaiming their bodies and their illnesses from 'modernist medicine'. If, in modern societies, medicine colonized the body and illness, and effectively silenced the patient's experience, by subjecting it to the categories and control of medical thought, now lay people can adopt a 'post-colonial' or 'postmodern stance', such that they can articulate their views without necessarily referring to medicine and physicians at all (Frank 1995: 13). Whereas in Frank's earlier discussion the emphasis was partly on the shortcomings of health care staff in reacting to illness, the later work focuses on the layperson's efforts to refashion life with illness as an integral component, rather than with illness denied. This helps explain the recent attention to patient narratives, in sociology and outside it, where the heterogeneity of experience is given full expression, and where it is contrasted with the more technical and scientific view of illness in 'evidence-based' medicine (Bury 2001).

Developing his argument in *At the Will of the Body*, and taking on board Kleinman's approach to illness narratives, Frank suggests that sociology, like medicine, needs to adopt a stance of being a witness to suffering by listening to such narratives (Frank 1995: 24). In this way, social science and medicine can both be situated, he argues, in a new 'ethics of the body' (p. 24). A number of considerations follow from this stance. One of these concerns the question of loss which illness often involves. Illness, Frank contends, is invariably accompanied by a loss of desire, for the mundane (buying clothes, having one's teeth taken care of) as well as for the more important things in life. But, in the new culture described by Frank, illness can also be the opportunity to reflect on the nature of desire and, under some circumstances, find alternative pleasures and sources of positive feelings toward others (p. 40). Illness narratives that give expression to such efforts are the means of repairing damage to the body and the self, and facing the future; 'of re-drawing maps and finding new destinations' (p. 53).

Frank presents a compelling case for rethinking the relationship between the body and the experience of illness in contemporary 'postmodern' cultures. It is also clear from his writings, and from their reception, that they resonate with the experience of many patients and their families. For some sociologists, too, the prospect of exploring how laypeople 'transcend' the loss involved in illness, and reintegrate the body and self on a different level, hold particular attractions (Charmaz 2000: 287). At the very least, such an approach helps to overcome the tendency to rely only on documenting the negative experiences of patients. However, for others, the emphasis in Frank's work on 'restitution', 'chaos' and 'quest' narratives (the latter involving a 'journey' through illness to a new way of living), when linked with the 'ethic' of witness, carries with it strong religious overtones (G. Williams 1998; Bury 2001). It suggests a form of 'redemption through suffering', and as such may have more problematic connotations. In particular, it implies that health is a matter of 'ongoing moral self-transformation' in which both 'public and private performances are constantly required' (Clarke et al. 2003: 172).

In the viewpoint developed by Frank, health and illness, mind and body, and the natural and the social are couched in 'holistic' terms rather than as interactive. Indeed, towards the end of *The Wounded Storyteller*, Frank speaks of the 'communicative body' pursuing an incomplete project (Frank 1995: 164), which, echoing those who profess a faith, involves a situation where 'recursive processes continuously loop, never conclude'. Whilst for some laypeople such a 'project' may be life-enhancing and positive, for others it may prove less appealing, especially in the face of the attraction of a secularized way of approaching pain and suffering, such as 'bracketing it off' and minimizing its impact on self-identity, or in relying more on 'modernist' medical treatment. An emphasis on 'narration' and 'constructed' selfhood needs to be explored carefully, if only to examine the variations in experience which may be found in relation to these different responses to illness and the body. An emphasis on 'narratives' and 'journeys' may also leave the sociological imagination wondering where social structures and social divisions have gone, as subjectivity becomes the focus of attention, at the expense of situating illness in everyday material circumstances and in the social actions of those involved. The insights that Frank brings to the experience of illness and the body express some of the possible weaknesses of a sociology of 'embodiment', as well as its humanitarian strengths, a matter to which the chapter returns in the final section. First, however, the question of disability and the body needs to be considered.

The Challenges of Disability and the Body

Frank's work on illness narratives and the body attempts to give expression to a wide range of experience including that of disability as well as illness. The inclusion of disability in Frank's discussion presumes, as many other discussions do, that disability can first and foremost be seen as an alteration to the body and its functioning. In the USA, and particularly in the UK in recent years, however, a very different approach to disability and the body has emerged. As was noted in chapter 1, in the USA the phrase 'people with disabilities' is still widely used, even by those active in the disability movement, expressing the view that disability is a property of the individual; it is something to be lived *with*. In the UK this approach has been rejected by a number of influential disability activists, who have argued for a quite different approach. This new approach has a number of implications for how the body, health and society should be thought about and acted upon. It raises once more the tension between health as an attribute of the person and health as a relation of self with others.

The most important feature of the 'radical' approach to disability is its rejection of both medical and sociological conceptualizations. Medical approaches, whether in terms of definitions and measures of disability used in public health research (where attempts are made to assess the size and nature of disability in a given community or country) or in terms of more clinical applications in the treatment and rehabilitation of people with disabling conditions such as stroke or arthritis, are rejected as the basis for understanding disability. Likewise, sociological approaches which stress the experiential side of living with disability, or the meanings and narratives that are attached to different conditions, are equally found wanting. Both approaches, it is argued, individualize disability and see it as inherent in the body, and have therefore underpinned the 'social oppression' of disabled people, leading to discrimination and social exclusion. In opposition to this, a particular approach to social relations and disability is advocated, which distances itself from the physical attributes of individuals.

In a series of publications, disability activists in the UK have argued strenuously for such a view. Perhaps the best-known writing in this vein has been that of Oliver (1990, 1996). For Oliver, a truly 'social model' of disability would cease to regard it as a consequence of altered or damaged bodies, whether as the result of illness or of trauma, and instead see it as a product of features of the physical and social environment which lead to social exclusion. Official definitions of disability, Oliver argues, deflect attention from these issues and concentrate instead on the incapacities ('what is wrong') with the person (Oliver 1990: 7). Instead, he argues, disability should be redefined in terms of what is wrong with society, rather than what is wrong with the individual, thus turning the tables on the social oppression of disabled people. Medicalizing disability, or concentrating attention on subjective meanings attached to bodily change as some sociological work does, are equally guilty in this view. They direct attention away from the real sources of difficulty of disabled people: namely, the 'disabling' features of contemporary society.

What is involved here is a separation of bodily change, often referred to in the mainstream medical and disability literature as 'impairment', from disability, defined as restricted activity and participation. Complex arguments have been raging across the international disability field in recent years on how to reconcile official definitions and their operationalizion in research, with more radical impulses (Bury 2000b). For some the matter can be expressed more cogently and simply. Oliver, for example, has argued that 'the social model insists, disablement is nothing to do with the body. It is a consequence of social oppression' (Oliver 1996: 35). Impairment, on the other hand, is related to the body, as it is 'nothing less than a description of the physical body' (p. 35). What Oliver is arguing is that whilst impairment, or illness, can have effects on social life, and can, under certain conditions, be properly treated as bodily ailments by medicine, 'disability as a long term social state is not treatable medically' (p. 36). Taken to its logical conclusion, the 'social model' of disability insists on focusing firmly on social conditions as separate from impairment and individual experience, and from medical care.

Defining disability wholly in terms of social conditions and practices that either enhance or inhibit participation, and separating it from the 'differences' which impairments entail, provides the basis, so it is argued, for concentrating on social and political action to combat discrimination.

In recent years, however, a reaction to the argument for the strict separation of impairment and disability has been occurring. Debates among sociologists and disability activists have led to a number of different positions being put forward about the relationship between body, disability and society. As far as disability activists are concerned, Barnes and Mercer (2003) provide a useful summary of some of these views. Their starting point is similar to that of Oliver, reiterating the charge that the sociology of chronic illness has been overly concerned with impairments and their subjective meanings. An emphasis on loss and the repair of biographical integrity is regarded as too individualistic in tone. This threatens, to 'undermine the social model's political project', they argue. By contrast, the benefit of the 'social model' of disability, Barnes and Mercer contend, is that it concentrates attention on challenging 'outside' environmental forces that create a disabling society. Even so, some of the arguments they summarize and develop suggest that a more 'eclectic' approach may be 'compelling' (p. 66).

In the first place, they consider the possibility that bodily impairments in and of themselves can be 'oppressive' in character. The pain, distress and uncertainty that the onset of symptoms or the occurrence of impairments can bring are an important part of the reality that disabled people live with. In this sense the analysis makes implicit connections with the approach to pain and loss discussed above in the work of Frank. Moreover, following the work of writers such as French (1993) and Thomas (1999), Barnes and Mercer accept that impairments matter to people, and that they can have outcomes which no change in social structure can affect. The most obvious example is that of not being able to drive as the result of visual impairment (2003: 72). Whilst the social model might redirect attention from the ability to drive, to tackle the need for alternative means of transport and 'inclusion' for those who cannot do so, this does not get around the inability to drive as such, or whether this is experienced in terms of the loss or absence of pleasure or independence for the individual.

Second, Barnes and Mercer attempt to integrate some of the insights from the sociology of chronic illness into their discussion. Here they draw on the work of Bury (1988) among others. This work on chronic illness has distinguished between the meaning of illness or impairment in terms of its consequences and the meaning in terms of its significance. The 'consequences' of illness refer to the practical matters that have to be confronted, in dealing with an altered body in an environment that may or may not be supportive. Everyday activities and routines in the home may have to be reorganized, and the demands of the working environment may prove excessive. The 'significance' of a disorder relates to how visible it is, which part of the body is affected, and how these issues are located within a particular culture. Barnes and Mercer link this last point to the need to recognize that 'disability' as conceptualized in the more radical 'social model' has often been seen as a set of common experiences that cut across different illnesses and impairments. But impairments often carry specific connotations – consider, for example, the different implications for social interaction of being without sight or without hearing or speech – bringing to the fore the need to recognize variation and diversity among disabled people (Barnes and Mercer 2003: 79).

Lastly, Barnes and Mercer recognize that much of the disability activists' attachment to the 'social model' has tended to reproduce a sharp division between mind and body – the Cartesian dualism – discussed earlier in this chapter. There is something of an irony here, if only because many disability activists, like some sociologists, have been at pains to castigate 'positivistic science', whether medical or sociological, for its presumed 'reductionism' and dualistic character. This chapter has also alluded to such 'dualism' in areas such as feminist thinking, which separate biological characteristics from socially organized roles. Yet Barnes and Mercer recognize that the 'social model' of disability has equally separated off the body from social arrangements, in order to concentrate its fire on social discrimination and exclusion. In so doing it has conceptualized the body in neutral terms, as simply the passive or neutral repository of 'impairment'. All these considerations lead Barnes and Mercer to conclude by embracing an approach to disability based on a 'sociology of embodiment' (p. 85), which brings together the subjective experiences of individuals and the broader contexts in which they occur.

This more integrated approach has also been developing among medical sociologists, who have likewise been interested in according greater recognition to the body in discussions of chronic illness and disability. Two brief examples will suffice to conclude this section of the discussion. The first is that of Kelly and Field (1996). In their paper on chronic illness and the body, Kelly and Field argue that identity develops in human beings through an interaction of the self and the wider society. Identity, here, is the outcome of a series of complex relays between physical appearance, behaviours and 'outside definitions' concerning such matters as age, gender and ethnicity (Kelly and Field 1996: 245). Crucial to becoming 'competent social performers' in society is the ability to 'give the impression of some degree of control, use and presentation of our bodies' (p. 246). The presence or onset of chronic illness or disability threatens to compromise this social 'performance' – located within a set of social and cultural expectations and demands – and leads to a series of implications for 'self-management'. In the case of a disorder such as diabetes, self-management practices may remain hidden, but in the case of someone in a wheelchair, these are visible as part of the person's public identity (p. 249). In this way, self-identity, body and society are best seen, again, as a set of dynamic processes. The demands of the 'outside' social environment and the nature of the distribution of resources are clearly of importance here.

The second example is that of G. Williams (2001) who has drawn attention to the value of the work of the American medical sociologist and disability activist Irving Zola, who tried through his life and work to reconcile a rejection of disability as a matter of 'individual tragedy' with an attention to 'lived experience'. For Zola, the term 'people with disabilities' recognizes both the commonality of experience and its diversity. In particular, Williams argues, Zola's attention to the question of ageing and disability (almost entirely absent in most disability activists' writing on the subject) shows how the interests of the 'disabled' and the 'able-bodied' could be linked. However important it may be to identify the political interests of disabled people as a 'minority group' in fighting 'social oppression', it is, Zola argued, a curious minority. It will, after all, include all of us, 'if not today, then tomorrow, or the day after' (G. Williams 2001: 139). We are all likely to have to contend with the processes that involve changes to our bodies, and with negotiating the different meanings of disability in different social settings at different points in the lifecourse. Such considerations warn against underplaying either biological or social factors in producing and shaping disability.

Critiques of the Body in Sociology

This chapter has sought to illustrate the ways in which a sociology of the body, or 'embodiment', has the potential to illuminate different aspects of health. Three approaches have been explored: the interaction of body and society in producing particular health outcomes across the lifecourse; the experience of health and the body, through 'illness narratives' in giving shape and human expression to the processes at work; and the controversy surrounding chronic illness and disability when seen in terms of 'embodiment'. Though tensions and disagreements have been noted, the main argument has been that exploring connections between the body, health and society is a productive way of developing a sociological understanding of the issues involved.

However, not all sociologists agree with this view. Criticisms of focusing on the body have been recently advanced within sociology, and these should be noted by way of a brief final section to the chapter. Perhaps the most cogent expression of a sceptical view has been in a recent paper by Howson and Inglis (2001). These authors begin by noting two possible currents of thought that help explain the growing interest in the sociology of the body. The first of these is the emergence of a more 'interdisciplinary' approach to academic study, in an attempt to overcome the 'dualisms' of mind and body, subject and object (Howson and Inglis 2001: 298). Earlier comments about seeing the body and health as a dynamic interplay between the biological and the social exemplify this impulse in research and theorizing, as does the debate between medical sociology and disability studies. Second, Howson and Inglis argue that the sociology of the body has articulated a more 'reflexive' approach in sociological enquiry, which has led away from more 'objectivist' approaches, towards emphasizing subjective 'lived experience' (p. 298). This, it is argued, brings sociology closer to everyday reality and makes it less reliant on abstraction and theory, producing a situation in which what is involved in 'doing sociology' is reconceptualized. Overcoming dualisms and being more reflexive about sociological enquiry suggest a more engaged, less 'positivistic' approach to sociology.

Although Howson and Inglis state that they are 'broadly sympathetic' to these developments, they argue that they run the risk of leading analysis away from 'an adequate account of social structure' (p. 299). Such a tension was noted above – for example, in how far to conceptualize illness and disability in terms of narratives of the body and self-identity, and how far to concentrate on discrimination and 'oppression'. Howson and Inglis point out that Frank's analysis of the body, self and society, which emphasizes a 'view from below', is in marked contrast to the analyses of writers such as Turner (1996), where a 'top-down view' of the body shows it being caught in a web of regulation and restriction, and thus features of society's power structures (Howson and Inglis 2001: 301). The more subjective turn, they argue, takes sociology towards a more philosophical, 'phenomenological approach' to social life, in which the interplay of subject and object, or agency and structure, are marginalized. The emphasis on 'lived experience' in many contemporary approaches to the body are seen, here, to sacrifice key sociological issues such as 'accounts of power relations' and the more 'objective structures of power that *sociologically* are crucial in understanding any phenomenon' (Howson and Inglis 2001: 308, emphasis in the original).

Howson and Inglis's paper produced a number of responses from writers who have been advocating more explicit attention to the body or 'embodiment' in sociology. In the present context two of these responses are worth noting. The first is that of Shilling (2001), who repeats his argument that many classical sociological theorists have dealt implicitly with the body, and by bringing this out more clearly, their approaches to the constitution of society can be strengthened rather than weakened. For example, Shilling draws attention to the role of the body in Durkheim's work, especially that on religion, where 'the natural properties of the body provide a basis for symbolising that which defines social groups' (Shilling 2001: 332). The experience of the body allows individuals to recognize others 'as participants in social life' (p. 333). Social cohesion and social networks involve tolerance and acceptance of the physical presence and proximity of others as part of one's social world. Thus the collective aspects of social structure are rooted, in this argument, in Durkheim's preoccupation with the 'prohibitions and imperatives, that surround the body'. From this viewpoint there is no necessary antagonism between focusing on the body or on the wider society.

Second, Crossley (2001) takes up the charge that a redirection of sociology towards 'lived experience' involves a lack of attention to social structure and an erosion of the boundary between sociology and philosophy. Crossley attempts to rebut such arguments by showing that some of the most important thinkers on phenomenology and the body, such as Merleau-Ponty, retained a clear conception of the 'higher structures' of society and history. Like Durkheim's work, Crossley argues, such thought recognizes the 'manifest dynamics' of social structures which are 'strictly irreducible' to the individual or psychological level (Crossley 2001: 320). The approach to 'lived experience' in this form of phenomenology recognizes the importance of social contexts and their constraining character, but suggests that contexts themselves are produced by social actors, not simply 'outside' influences upon them. Just as human beings must conform to the rules of a given language in order to make sense in communication, so they modify it over time, 'intersubjectively' (p. 321). In this view, again, pitching subjective experience of the body against 'external' social structures is seen to be unnecessary, as each has an effect on the other.

Finally, then, fears that the sociology of the body, or of 'embodiment', take the analysis either too far towards an individual level of analysis (whether biological or psychological) or too far towards a preoccupation with subjective 'lived experience' (for example, in 'illness narratives') have received critical attention. Those opposed to focusing on the body have made their views of the importance of social structures and power clear. Replies have stressed how far the body is involved in the creation, maintenance and change of structures and their effects. From this viewpoint there is no need for further calls to 'bring the body back in' to sociological enquiry. What is involved when this happens is well under way, at least in British mainstream sociological debate, and in some sections of North American scholarship.

As far as medical sociology is concerned, with its focus on health and illness, it is clear that the body and 'embodiment' are likely to be of lasting concern. As elsewhere in this book, a 'dynamic' approach to the body, self and society is suggested. This involves recognizing that each area of human experience can have an independent and sometimes determining influence on the other. The body does not just set limits to social action, it can often have a determining effect on it. Poor maternal health or poor nutrition and, of course, disease can all have demonstrable effects, some immediate and some long-lasting across the lifecourse. The source of such events may sometimes be social, sometimes not, as in the case of genetic or 'idiopathic' illness (where there is no known cause). By the same token, social structures cannot exert their influence, whether seen as 'external' to the individual or not, without implications for human action and the human body. As in the example of disability, attempts to separate the body from the constraining influences of the social structure run into difficulty, because the constraints being discussed arise in relation to bodily processes. The latter cannot be treated as 'separate' or 'neutral' in any satisfactory sociological account. Whilst the body, self and society can all have their independent effects, each is influenced by the other, and all involve human agency. The study of health and illness remains one of the most fruitful ways of exploring these dynamics empirically.

Concluding Remark

The body is central to the understanding and experience of illness. Behind many of the medical and epidemiological depictions of health and illness lie bodies in pain and distress. The sociology of the body can help in understanding the processes at work, both biological and social, that lead to the occurrence and patterning of health and illness. But it can also attend to the impact that changes to the body through illness experience have on social life, both for self and others. This sociology of embodiment resonates particularly with changes in 'postmodern' cultures, in which subjective experience is given more emphasis. At the same time debates in areas such as disability show that tensions between subjectivity and the wider structural sources of inequality are of importance. Mainstream sociology has contributed to the development of work on health and illness, by 'bringing the body back in' to social analysis; but research on health and illness has been able to explore both its strengths and its weaknesses. The body and 'embodiment' are now central parts of sociological enquiry, and act as important links between health, illness, self and society.

5

Health and Health Care

So far in this book, the discussion of health has focused on its patterning and framing within a social context, and on its experiential dimension as it affects groups and individuals as social beings. The patterning of health refers to the many factors that can influence the occurrence and distribution of illness. 'Framing' refers, here, to the many forms (of knowledge and belief) which human agency creates in order to understand how health is maintained and how it goes wrong, and how to manage disorder when it does occur. The debates about health, disability and the body in the last chapter illustrated some of the complexities of patterning and framing in just one area of current controversy. Throughout the discussion of this and other health-related issues in the book, a dynamic perspective has been taken, indicating the changing nature of health and its framing over time, and the interaction of different influences on health and illness, whether biological, environmental or more broadly social.

But what of health care? Health services are not the only sites at which the experience of illness is played out, but they are frequently important when self-care no longer suffices. In modern times, formal health care services have become a central part of welfare systems. In the USA, the UK and other developed countries, a great deal of money is invested, and many hundreds of thousands of people are employed, in delivering health care, every hour of the day and every week of the year. In the UK at the end of the last century there were some 100,000 physicians, and in the USA no fewer than 800,000 (Porter 2002a: 44). Most European countries spend somewhere in the region of 7–9 per cent of gross domestic product on health, and the USA spends nearly 15 per cent (in 2002/3 the British NHS cost around £68 billion). In developing countries, personnel levels and expenditures of these magnitudes can only be dreamt of, despite the presence of major health problems.

Whether affordable or not, there is a general consensus that good-quality health care, available to all citizens is, or should be, a key priority for governments. Though countries differ markedly on how health care is funded – largely through the private sector in the USA, and through taxation in the UK – health care remains highly valued, by both providers and recipients alike. Even though no one looks forward to a stay in hospital, most communities value the health care facilities that are available to them, and will often campaign vigorously if they are threatened with reduction or closure. Health care stands between the individual and some of the most serious personal experiences that can occur across the lifecourse, whether they relate to birth, ill health or death. Not surprisingly, therefore, surveys of public opinion have frequently shown high levels of overall satisfaction with existing health care provision. No one wishes to see such provision diminished or downgraded.

However, if we step back for a moment, key questions about the relationship between health and health care present themselves. These can be grouped together under three broad headings, and these form the basis of the discussion in this chapter. The first set of questions concerns the impact of health care on health, when viewed from a population standpoint. To remind the reader, the population, or public health, view is concerned less with the role of health care in dealing with individual illness episodes, and more with the longer-term effects of health care on whole communities. The second set of questions deals with the effectiveness of health care at the more individual level, and is concerned with the evaluation of health care and the production of systematic evidence on its outcomes, both good and bad. The third and final set of questions deals with what might be called the 'social relations of health care', especially the nature of professional – patient encounters and how they have changed in recent years.

Health Care and Populations

At first sight, the relationship between the health of populations and the provision of health care seems straightforward. In most developed countries measures of population health have shown a steady improvement over many decades. Two of the measures most often used illustrate the point clearly. At the beginning of the last century, average life expectancy at birth in the UK was around 45 years for males and 49 years for females. This average was kept low as the result of high levels of infant and early adult life mortality caused by infectious diseases. By contrast, males and females born today can expect to live for 75 and 80 years respectively (ONS 2002). Similarly, as noted in chapter 1, the infant mortality rate (that is, deaths occurring in the first year of life), which is a powerful indicator of the social as well as biological conditions of mothers, fell in the UK from 24 to 6 per thousand live births between 1950 and 2000 (Gray 2001: 29). Many disorders which threatened life in the early and middle years have now been brought under control. In broad terms, people are healthier across the lifecourse, suffer fewer infectious illnesses (though, again, HIV/AIDS reminds us of the effects these can have on populations), and are increasingly healthy in adult life and early old age, though chronic and disabling disorders increase in later life.

At the same time, health care systems have grown and expanded in terms of the range of treatments on offer. Antibiotics are frequently thought to have been responsible for holding back if not conquering infectious disease, and safer forms of hospital-based childbirth and surgery appear to keep babies and adults alive more effectively than ever. Many disorders that were untreatable in the past can now be tackled. Common sense seems to dictate, therefore, that health care has been largely responsible for the improvement in the population's health, and few doctors have sought to challenge the assumptions on which such a popular perception is based. If modern medicine is thought to be responsible for improvements in health, then the prestige of doctors is enhanced.

Yet the evidence for the relationship between health care and improvements in population health is more equivocal. Perhaps the best known of all critiques of the role of medicine in human health has been that of Thomas McKeown, professor of social medicine at the University of Birmingham in the UK from 1945 to 1977. In a detailed study of the historical changes in population health in England, from the mid-nineteenth century (when the recording of the causes of death began) until the 1970s, McKeown (1979) showed that in many cases the role of medicine in observed improvements was negligible. The clearest example was that of tuberculosis, one of the most important causes of death in the nineteenth and early twentieth centuries, as it still is in parts of the developing world today. McKeown showed that mortality from tuberculosis was already declining before the tubercle bacillus was identified as its cause in the early 1880s, and had declined even further before chemotherapy (in the shape of streptomycin) was introduced in 1948 (McKeown 1979: 92–3). A large part of the improvement in mortality from tuberculosis therefore had little or nothing to do with health care.

McKeown's discussion dealt with a range of infectious diseases as well as tuberculosis, and though this was the most dramatic example, a similar picture was shown for many others. The improvement in the health of populations and the rise in health care and in modern medicine were largely coincidental. Most of the many thousands of treatments which doctors provided in early modern medicine, up to the 1930s and 1940s, were ineffective, with the exception, perhaps, of medicaments such as quinine for malaria and opium as an analgesic. As the medical historian Roy Porter has put it, 'true cures remained elusive, however, and doctors knew that their prescriptions were largely eyewash' (Porter 2002a: 39).

McKeown, however, was keen to note examples where, in the post-Second World War period at least, medical treatments helped to keep rates of infection down. In addition, in cases such as that of poliomyelitis, immunization had been responsible for major gains. Nevertheless, the brunt of McKeown's thesis on the role of medicine and health care suggested that, overall, it had been limited historically. Even where the decline in mortality could be related to medical treatment, as in diphtheria, for example, McKeown stressed that other factors must also have been present. For McKeown, these other influences, resulting from progressively higher levels of economic and social development, had as important an effect on population health as health care, if not greater. The most obvious was the improvement to the physical environment, in terms of the provision of clean, safe drinking water and the disposal of sewage. Changes in health-related behaviour were also important, especially the development of contraception which helped to limit family size, reducing risks to both mothers and the babies that were born. But insufficient and poor-quality nutrition was seen to be, and remained for McKeown, the 'most important determinant of health' McKeown (1979: 119). Although he admitted that the direct historical evidence for this contention was limited, he argued that, when combined with environmental change and limiting family size, there could be little doubt of its importance, given what was then known about the role of proper nutrition in promoting health (p. 60).

The implications of McKeown's thesis on the historically limited role of medicine in the improvement of health in populations are dramatic. They show that health care is not the sole determinant of health, and under certain conditions not the most important one in influencing the health of communities. In developed societies such as the USA and the UK, non-health care factors, such as changes in behaviour in reducing smoking, or adopting a more healthy diet and engaging in more exercise, may be more important than relying on medicine to find cures, especially in an era dominated by 'degenerative' diseases such as heart disease and cancer – that is, diseases associated with greater longevity. The

McKeown thesis also has clear implications for developing countries, where the provision of clean water, sewage disposal, adequate nutrition and contraception all continue to present important challenges. It is clear that reliance on high-tech health care, even if it can be afforded, does not have any linear relationship to the level of health of populations, and that non-medical actions remain important. McKeown's thesis on the role of health care continues to have widespread salience.

But the matter cannot be left there, and McKeown's thesis needs to be revisited in the changed circumstances of the last 30 years. Two caveats, in particular, must be entered in any consideration of McKeown's thesis, and the theses of others who argue a similar case on the limited role of modern medicine in tackling population health. The first concerns the role of economic and social development. As critics such as Szreter (2001) have pointed out, McKeown's own reservations about the lack of direct evidence on the role of nutrition were well founded. Szreter argues that nutrition arises as an important factor in McKeown's thesis by default – it is taken to be of crucial importance because of the 'sceptical devaluation of other factors including medical interventions, rather than because of any convincing positive evidence in its favour' (Szreter 2001: 222). Improvements in nutrition are taken to be part of overall economic development, acting as a general impetus towards better living standards and thus better health.

The difficulty with this approach to the links between society and health, Szreter argues, is that it rests on a 'hidden hand' model of development, as if positive changes occur without human agency and without political struggle and division. In fact, Szreter shows that in the UK, public health measures – especially sanitary reforms – rather than the direct effects of nutrition, were central to improving health. These reforms, in turn, were critically dependent on local public health pioneers enacting legislation such as the 1878 Public Health (Water) Act and the Sale of Food and Drugs Act of 1899, often involving major political conflict at local and regional municipal levels. Far from being the result of general, undirected 'improvement' in economic and social conditions, such changes came about as a result of concerted human agency. Szreter's argument is that McKeown failed to appreciate the nature of national, and especially local, actions and the political conflicts that often surrounded them. Szreter also implies that, as in the past, if improvements in public health are to be pursued in the future, human agency within specific communities is an important requirement.

The second caveat concerns the tendency to read from McKeown's thesis the lesson that health care today still has little or nothing to contribute to the population's health. This needs to be treated with caution, for at least two reasons. First, and as McKeown himself noted, the reduction in mortality from infectious diseases has been helped by the advent of effective drugs such as antibiotics, which have kept levels to a minimum. Even in developing countries, governments and health care systems are not in the same position as in nineteenth-century England, in that they can employ *both* public health measures *and* modern medicaments. Argument concerning anti-viral drugs for HIV/Aids in Africa is a case in point. The choices here are more complex than in a period where little by way of effective treatment was available. It also needs to be remembered that effective public health measures, including interventions such as vaccination programmes, which continue to have such dramatic and positive effects world-wide (for example, in polio, which is now close to being eradicated in many countries), are the result of scientific medical understanding. Though the application of such understanding is, in this case, at a public health level, individuals clearly benefit from its effects.

Secondly, and related to the last point, health care, like health, needs to be treated as a dynamic phenomenon. Whilst McKeown's thesis was developed against a backdrop of modern medicine up to the mid-1970s, much has changed in the intervening period. Many forms of clinical intervention today are increasingly effective, to the extent that positive effects on public health, as well as on the health of individuals, are beginning to be felt. Douglas Black, for example, has distinguished between health conditions that are 'amenable' and those that are 'non-amenable' to treatment in this respect (Black 1994). He argues, on the basis of evidence from a number of European countries and from North America, that the treatment of 'amenable' diseases (such as some forms of heart disease and cancer) is having an appreciable effect on survival, but its wider impact on population health is masked because statistics are combined with the treatment of other more intractable and chronic conditions.

Data on medical effectiveness from the USA have been analysed by Bunker (2001). In his estimation, treatment for conditions such as appendicitis, diabetes, tuberculosis, infant respiratory failure and end-state renal failure are making appreciable contributions to improved life expectancy. Bunker estimates that, 'all told, clinical services, composed of preventive services as well as therapeutic intervention, can be credited with five or five and a half of the thirty year increase in life expectancy since 1900, and as much as half of the 7.6 years of increase in life expectancy since 1950' (Bunker 2001: 42). This contribution of medical treatment to population health will, in all likelihood, continue in the future. Compared to the historical period examined by McKeown, we have now entered a phase where the difference between treating individuals and improving the health of the public are increasingly difficult to separate. As clinical treatments of individuals (especially for common disorders) become more effective, the more they are likely to contribute to the health of whole communities. Thus, evaluating the effects of health care, even at the level of the outcome of clinical treatment of individuals, takes on an increasingly important role for society as a whole, as well as for individual patients.

Evaluating Health Care

The idea of evaluating the effectiveness of health care at the level of the individual is not new. However, the acceptance that medical treatments should be put to the test scientifically has long been fraught with difficulties. As Sir Richard Doll (the epidemiologist responsible for establishing the link between smoking and lung cancer) stated in a recent article in which he looked back over a long medical career, 'When I qualified in medicine in 1937, new treatments were almost always introduced on the grounds that in the hands of professor A or in the hands of a consultant at one of the leading teaching hospitals, the results in a small series of patients (seldom more than 50) had been superior to those recorded by professor B (or some other consultant) or by the same investigator previously' (Doll 1998: 1217). In other words, the clinical judgement of the individual practitioner held sway, and few were able or willing to challenge it, even when they thought it misplaced. Most routine treatments in the health services then, and to a lesser extent now, have never been evaluated on a scientific basis. In everyday experience in clinics and hospitals, either the patient survived or not, or appeared to get better or not. In many cases, the practitioner would not know what the long-term outcomes of the treatment in question were.

As with McKeown's challenge to assumptions about the impact of health care on populations, the 1970s witnessed another major assault on medical (and public) complacency concerning health care. This time, the challenge was to clinical medicine to deal with the absence of good-quality evidence on the effectiveness (that is, the clinical results or outcomes) of treatment. In a path-breaking book that is still having an impact across the world, Cochrane's *Effectiveness and Efficiency: Random Reflections on Health Services* (1972) set out the need to subject medical treatments to proper evaluation. Cochrane gave a number of examples of established and popular treatments for which evidence of effectiveness was lacking. Perhaps the most dramatic of his claims at the time was his assertion that there was no evidence of 'any medical gain in admission to hospital with coronary care units compared with treatment at home' (Cochrane 1972: 29). Cochrane described a similar situation for a number of other conditions, other than heart attacks. Well-established therapies were not, by virtue of their long popularity, necessarily well founded in terms of effectiveness.

Cochrane's answer to this dilemma was to advocate the use of randomized controlled trials (RCTs) in which patients would be allocated to two groups: the treatment, or new treatment, group and the control group, which might be an existing treatment or a placebo (that is, a non-therapeutic treatment). At the end of the period of study, the outcomes for the two groups would be compared, to see which had fared better. In order to get round the problem that the practitioner might know which patients were receiving the treatment being tested, and thus introduce a potential bias into the evaluation, patients would be allocated by a statistical procedure (for example, by using random numbers to decide which group a patient would be allocated to), and the process would be managed by a remote investigator, rather than the practitioner concerned. In this way a neutral check on the administration of the treatment could be set in place.

Although Cochrane argued that many routine treatments and new innovations could be evaluated in this way, he could see the difficulties in advocating that RCTs should be applied to *all* areas of health service activity. For example, where a procedure is the only available treatment and the condition is life-threatening, random allocation might simply mean death for some patients. Surgery for lung cancer is a case in point. Similarly, in many cases the outcome of treatment is difficult to define and agree upon – for example, in many instances of mental health. Where there is no consensus about outcome, then testing effectiveness is bound to be hampered, if not impossible. The ambiguity of this situation was not lost on Cochrane. In these kinds of situations, he argued, such treatment meant that 'patients' interests are very well protected and on the other hand that there are sections of medicine whose effectiveness cannot at present be measured' (Cochrane 1972: 23–4).

In the years since 1972, the assimilation of Cochrane's ideas has brought about significant change in medical thought. The 'Cochrane Collaboration' now comprises a world-wide network of scientists and practitioners dedicated to conducting systematic evaluations of medical treatments, often through the use of RCTs, and bringing the findings to bear on what is now referred to as 'evidence-based health care'. The idea behind this is to bring together, and attempt to integrate, 'clinical expertise and the best external evidence', to use the phrase of one of its most enthusiastic proponents (Sackett et al. 1996: 71). As Fitzpatrick (2004) points out, bodies such as the National Institute of Clinical Excellence in the UK, and similar organizations in other countries, now have a central role in providing authoritative statements about the effectiveness of treatments, to guide practice and to determine whether these should be provided in publicly funded health services.

Important though these developments are, issues concerning human agency and the social context of evaluation once more raise significant sociological questions, and these take us to the heart of health care delivery. Two brief points will indicate just some of the issues involved.

The first of these concerns the relationship between clinical practice and scientific evidence. Whilst the arguments of writers such as Doll, Cochrane and Sackett have constituted an important critique of individual clinical judgements about what 'works', ordinary practitioners may regard the advocacy of scientific evaluation negatively. For many it may be seen as little more than an unwarranted move by a self-appointed academic elite within the profession. The tension between medical science and everyday practice has been a feature of the history of medicine from its earliest days. 'Evidence-based health care' can, therefore, be readily characterized as the latest attempt to create a new form of 'discourse' through which the elite can retain their privileged status. Armstrong (2002) has recently argued that, in the UK at least, the medical profession as a whole is constrained to adopt an 'evidence-based' approach to practice, to ward off challenges to its autonomy, especially from governments in their desire to regulate medicine and control costs. From the point of view of the general practitioner in particular, however, this may be experienced more as an increase in surveillance, with little appreciation of actual decision making about treatment on a day-to-day basis (Doust 2004). Part of the contradiction in the situation lies in the fact that health care providers are, at the same time, being persuaded to adopt a more 'patient-oriented' style of practice. As Armstrong argues, this alternative form of discourse offers general practitioners, somewhat ironically, a means with which to defend their case for resisting 'evidence-based practice' and retaining their independent judgement.

The second point concerns the patient in this changing pattern of health service delivery and evaluation. Patients, arguably, are no longer as passive as they once were, and may, indeed, have their own views of treatment and its effectiveness. They are likely increasingly to challenge doctors' views, whether evidence-based or not. Those advocating the use of scientific methods such as RCTs rarely discuss the patient's view of such procedures or their outcomes. It is assumed that this must be positive – who would resist more effective treatments? Yet, as Howitt and Armstrong (1999) have shown, even where patients are given the results of the latest evidence concerning effectiveness, they may not be willing to accept it. In their study of treatment for heart disease, it was found that a significant minority of patients did not want to change their treatment, even when offered a more 'effective' alternative. Instead, they preferred to stay with the tried and tested treatment they were already receiving. This was especially true among older patients. The acceptability of research evidence among patients is as important an issue as it is among practitioners.

As patients are enrolled in evaluation studies, and especially clinical trials, in ever larger numbers, the need to understand the patient viewpoint will become increasingly important. Not only will more and more patients have to give informed consent to such studies, but they will be asked, particularly as a result of random allocation, to undergo treatments that may not have any benefit for them as individuals. The attempt to evaluate medical treatments crosses the line between treating the patient *as* a patient and treating the patient as an experimental subject. As Featherstone and Donovan have clearly shown, this can involve a range of questions concerning the different understandings of the process held by the investigator and by the patient. For example, the term 'random' in random allocation means a neutral statistical device to the investigator, but may mean 'without any logic' to the layperson or patient (Featherstone and Donovan 2002). Confusion about what exactly is involved for patients in participating in RCTs, and in accepting the evidence they produce, is likely to become pronounced. Thus evidence-based medicine is feeding into a series of changes in the *process* of care (especially in the practitioner–patient relationship), as well as in its outcome.

Changes in the Social Relations of Health Care

Enough has already been said in this chapter to indicate that health care, like health itself, is a dynamic process, subject to change over time. The growing tensions within medicine between different groups of health care practitioners, and between the evaluation of treatment and responding to patients' views, as discussed above, reflect the different pressures bearing down on medicine from differing quarters. In this section of the chapter, three aspects of the context and process of contemporary health care are examined: the changing nature of medical decision making, the changing context of health care practice, and the changing character of health policy governing the shape of health care activities.

Decision making in health care

Until recently, sociological writing on decision making in health has been strongly influenced by Eliot Freidson's early analysis of 'medical dominance' (Freidson 1970/1988). Although Freidson was to change his position over the years, especially in the light of the rise of 'managed care' in the USA (see below), his critique of the extent of power of the medical profession over the patient has been widely influential. For Freidson the ability of the medical profession to decide what is and what is not illness (the power to label) and the effective exclusion of the patient's view of their illness in health care practice have meant that modern medicine has gained unchallenged dominance. The presence in the community of lay healing practices and lay networks of support and care, Freidson argued, went unnoticed in a period when hospital-based medicine gave increasing power to the medical profession over health and illness.

In the UK a series of studies seemed to lend support to Freidson's position, indicating that patients' subjective views of their illnesses were seen by practitioners, at best as a means of ensuring compliance, and at worst as an obstruction to 'proper decision making' – namely, that carried out by the doctor. The appropriate role of the patient from this viewpoint was to simply to 'obey doctors' orders' (Stimson 1974). Critiques of the role of medicine in decision making were particularly sharp in areas such as maternity care, where the medical profession had extended its power into an arena where lay knowledge was extensive (Oakley 1984). Numerous arguments ensued, on this and other topics, concerning the appropriate balance between technical medical expertise and the ever increasing influence of medicine on everyday life, and as an important instrument of social control (Zola 1972).

Carefully constructed qualitative studies suggested, however, that medical dominance was not always complete, and in many instances needed qualifying. Stimson and Webb (1975) had shown that patients often subverted medical control of decision making, and used a number of countervailing measures to redress the balance of power with doctors. Non-compliance and criticism of doctors *outside* the clinic setting were two such possibilities. Importantly, studies suggested that even in the clinic decision making was a negotiated process more than simply one of doctors knowing best and imposing their will.

Silverman (1987), for example, showed that whilst medical dominance over decision making could be observed in both public and private clinics in the UK, at least two qualifications were needed in order to present a rounded picture. The first of these, following Strong's earlier comparative study of American and UK hospitals (Strong 1979), referred to the 'ceremonial' nature of clinic encounters. This ensured that in one form or another, decision making was accompanied by a 'medical etiquette' involving the doctor listening as well as pronouncing. This meant that the patient could exert a degree of autonomy in the decision making process. Second, Silverman noted, especially in clinics where children were the patients, that doctors operated with a developed sense of 'theoreticity' – that is, with a judgement concerning the ability of the patient to understand and reason about the medical issues at stake, including participating in choices to be made between alternative courses of action (Silverman 1987: 212).

In recent years, the idea of shared or joint decision making has become more explicit and popular in policy circles, and has also become attractive to many doctors and patients. In a series of papers, Charles and her colleagues, working in Ontario, Canada, have sought to clarify what is meant by shared decision making, and how it can be seen as a dynamic process at the heart of health care (Charles et al. 1997, 1999). In essence, the shared decision making process is seen to stand between two other approaches to decision making: the paternalistic model and the informed model. Each has implications for the way in which clinic encounters are conducted and decisions arrived at. Charles et al. are at pains to emphasize that the three models are analytic constructs. In everyday clinical encounters, elements of all three 'may occur together or in an interactive way' (Charles et al. 1999: 652). They are briefly considered here.

The paternalistic model is, perhaps, the point of departure, in that it embodies the medical dominance central to health care systems in the past. According to Charles at al. (1999) this approach is characterized by information flowing one way (largely from doctor to patient). Such information is usually of a minimal amount, and often no more than what is regarded as being legally required. In this model doctors assume that they have the best interests of the patient in mind, and, because of their medical expertise, are best able to judge the costs and benefits to the patient of different treatment options (p. 652). Such an approach to decision making has been reinforced by the presence of strong professional codes of ethics, which have sought to ensure that doctors do indeed act in their patients' best interest.

As part of a reaction to paternalism, the informed model and the shared model have developed. The informed model has emphasized the fact that it is the patient who has to live with the consequences of decisions made in the clinic, and therefore it should be the patient who decides. In this model, according to Charles et al. (1999), information still comes largely from the doctor; but it differs from the paternalistic model in that all relevant information for decision making is provided. It is then the patient, alone or with others, who deliberates and finally decides to implement a treatment option or not (doing nothing is, of course, a decision in itself). In this model the doctor is relegated to the position of adviser and technician, carrying out the patient's expressed wishes.

In between the paternalistic and the informed patient models stands the shared decision making model, sometimes today referred to (in the

UK NHS, at least) as a feature of 'partnership' or 'concordance' (the latter replacing 'compliance' with respect to medicine taking) in health care. Shared decision making involves a two-way process of information giving and receiving, involving both medical and 'lay' knowledge about the condition and its treatment. Such information should, as in the informed patient model, be full and relevant to the decision making process. The doctor and patient (with others) should be at the centre of deliberations over treatment, and the final decision should be jointly arrived at by discussion and negotiation where necessary.

Whilst it is clear that the shared or partnership approach is now becoming the preferred view concerning relationships in modern health care systems, there are a number of considerations to be borne in mind as thinking on the issue develops. Perhaps the most important concerns the rhetorical character of terms such as 'concordance' or 'partnership' among proponents of shared approaches to decision making. Charles et al. (1999) make the point that empirical studies are needed in order to check on the value of such ideas in different medical settings, so that their relevance to practitioners and patients alike can be properly assessed. As with advocates of 'patient-oriented' medicine, while shared decision making is firmly on the new health care agenda (Coulter and Fitzpatrick 2000), it is less clear how attractive it actually is to different patient groups. There is a danger that new languages and concepts – forms of 'discourse' – are adopted in policy or professional circles as a means of appearing to devolve power to the patient while retaining actual control 'from above'.

Secondly, the ideas behind shared decision making may be based on a rather abstract view of 'the patient' or 'the patient's view'. Patients, like practitioners, come in many shapes and sizes, and a 'one size fits all' policy is unlikely to meet the needs of many individuals, who have a range of differing health-related problems. Older people and children, for example, are frequently part of family situations which limit individual autonomy, and where, therefore, decision making is likely to involve at least three individuals: the practitioner, the patient and the family member or carer. As Gabe et al. (2004) argue, the case of children in health care is an important one for thinking through issues concerning partnership, especially with respect to the different agendas each participant may bring to the medical encounter. Where a triad is involved, different forms of partnership may come into being as 'coalitions' are formed between any two of the three people concerned. The idea of shared decision making here has to be revised to take account of the different dynamics that may be actively set in train by the participants involved.

Finally, as Coulter (1999) has pointed out, advocacy of shared decision making and partnership has many implications for organizing and delivering health care, not least of which is that of resources. As will be clear from the discussion above, achieving shared decision making requires considerable time, as well as effort, on the part of all parties concerned. The provision of full information to the patient itself is easier to advocate than achieve. What would count as 'full information' about, for example, a medical treatment or surgical procedure, and at what point would the patient know that they had received full information? Moreover, the constraints on medical practice, including time and the need for a degree of equity between patients (Coulter 1999), means that there may be a tendency on the part of practitioners to fall back on more paternalistic forms of care, if only to make progress with particular matters in hand. Where illness is debilitating, or the source of fear and anxiety, such paternalism may sometimes be attractive to patients as well as doctors.

Changes in the context of health care

In addition to the above considerations of changes in ideology and practice in the processes of health care delivery, there are also major changes in the 'external' environment in which health care systems operate. These, too, operate to challenge 'medical dominance' and may influence the ways in which both patients and practitioners view ideas of partnership and shared decision making. The 'contestable culture' of which Giddens (1991) speaks is nowhere more evident than in health care, where many voices and agendas are currently heard or pursued. The era in which what doctors said was treated as revealed truth, if it ever existed in such a pure form, is now surely over. In its wake, voices and actions are emerging from many quarters, bringing new dynamics to bear on changes in health care. Space permits only brief comments on some of these.

The first is the acceleration of legal and regulatory frameworks governing medical practice. In the British NHS there were, until relatively recently, few opportunities available to patients to complain about the treatment they received or to claim damages when things went wrong. It was assumed, as noted above, that the doctor acted in the patient's best interest, and within a strict code of conduct. If the outcome of treatment was less than successful, or the patient died, this was rarely put down to medical error or incompetence, at least not publicly. The ethos surrounding health care was one of deference and gratitude on the part of the patient. If the physician or surgeon had done their best, then no more could reasonably be asked of them.

Today, patients now ask many more questions about their treatment and its outcomes, and decide for themselves whether to follow advice or not. Although a less reverential view of medical practice has been more evident in systems such as that in the USA, where private care and private insurance have held sway, challenges, complaints and questions are now as likely in publicly funded systems as in private ones. The British NHS, for example, now has internal complaints procedures for handling patients' concerns, and these are a part of a wider system of accountability and transparency in the NHS. I have noted elsewhere (Bury 1997: 105) that evidence of changes in this area were becoming apparent by the early 1990s, in increases in medical malpractice claims and in costs for doctors' membership of the Medical Defence Union, which provides insurance cover for UK doctors. A report by Dingwall et al. (1991) showed that as more consumerist and market-style relationships developed in the NHS, 'mutual liabilities' of patients and doctors were likely to be specified more formally.

Since then, a series of high-profile legal cases in the UK has heightened concerns about medical practice and individual doctors' behaviour and competence. Perhaps one of the most notable of these concerned the events surrounding a series of 29 deaths among children undergoing heart surgery at the Bristol Royal Infirmary between 1984 and 1985. Three doctors involved in the case were investigated in 1997 by the General Medical Council, which regulates and licenses medical practice in the UK. Two were struck off the register, and the third had restrictions placed on his surgical practice. Importantly, a public enquiry was set up to investigate the background to the events in Bristol and to make recommendations for changes in medical practice. Secrecy and arrogance among doctors were roundly criticized in the report, which drew on evidence from 577 witnesses, including 238 parents, and over 900,000 pages of documents. The enquiry took more than three years to complete its work (DoH 2001).

Such an unprecedented examination of doctors' conduct was accompanied by public demonstrations of anger directed at the individuals concerned. During the GMC hearings, large numbers of police were needed to ensure the safety of the three doctors as they entered and left the building – scenes unimaginable in earlier times. Subsequently, other high-profile cases received equally intense public attention, in areas such as the retention of human tissue for research by hospitals and in the vaccination of children, a matter which is discussed in more detail in chapter 6. Finally, and at a quite different level, the case of Harold Shipman, a general practitioner in Greater Manchester, who was found guilty in July 2000 of killing fifteen of his elderly patients (though it is estimated that he was responsible for the deaths of over 200), seemed to shatter once and for all the trust in doctors to work within ethical guidelines, and to be allowed continuing autonomy over their practice. Such autonomy is now subject to a host of legal, managerial and regulatory frameworks, which have further reduced doctors' claims to unchallenged 'medical dominance' (Gabe 2004).

As if this was not enough, the changing nature of mass media coverage of health and health care is creating a dynamic of its own, with considerable potential for changing medical practice. In the early days of radio and, later, television, the influence of the medical profession on its content was considerable (Karpf 1988), and programmes were couched in general health-promoting terms rather than providing specific medical information. Paternalism held that public provision of medical information about disease and its treatment would only raise patients' anxieties. Today medical information on disease and illness abounds, and in myriad conventional forms, from books and encyclopaedias to television and radio programmes, both factual and fictional (Bury and Gabe 1994). In such media coverage – especially in hospital 'soaps' – doctors now vie for a central place on-stage with nurses, managers and forensic psychologists.

In addition, health and health care information is available from many different sources. Nearly every clinical academic department has its own Internet site, and many provide patient guidelines on the treatment of different diseases. Patients can now access information at the click of a mouse about their medical conditions or about those of their family members or friends. A recent survey estimated that just under a quarter of Europeans and Americans had asked their doctor about a health problem after first reading about it on the Internet (Eaton 2002). Whilst commentators fear the danger of information overload and difficulty among lay people in being able or willing to use the information available, especially among poorer groups (Mead et al. 2003), its availability is growing by the day and may help to reshape professional–patient communication (Hardey 1999). It is important, of course, not to exaggerate this trend, especially as the use of the Internet is not universal. It also needs to be remembered that much of the information available on the Internet is produced by self-help groups and campaigning organizations, often acting jointly with medical experts. Whilst this 'shared' approach to medical information further weakens the boundaries between the worlds of the physician and those of the layperson, it paradoxically provides a new avenue for medical influence.

All these changes in the context of health care revolve round alterations in expectations and structures. Most patients no longer expect or want to be treated as children in a doctor–patient relationship characterized by paternalism. As Coulter (1999) puts it, patients have grown up, and doctors are going to have to get used to it. Patients and lay people can turn to alternative sources of information about their health, in order to check and possibly challenge what they are told by health care professionals, and are more likely to bring such information to bear in clinic encounters than they were in the past. Whilst dependence on doctors may be inevitable or even welcome for some, the general context of health care has changed to the point where such expectations are no longer the assumed norm.

The structural correlates of these changes relate to a pluralistic development in medical practice and health care provision more generally. Whilst this has been growing apace in the USA over a number of years, its development in centralized and publicly funded systems, such as that in the UK, is relatively recent. Even so, changes are occurring rapidly. The interrelation between new forms of media and health care are a case in point, with the advent, for example, of NHS Direct (a telephone-based information and help line run by nurses) and NHS online, an Internet site for NHS users in the UK.

In both the USA and the UK, the availability of what, until now, has been called 'alternative medicine' is widespread and growing. Porter (2002a) notes that 'at the end of the twentieth century there were more registered irregular healers in Britain than GPs, while in the USA, more visits were being paid to providers of unconventional therapy (425 million) than to primary care physicians (388 million)' (Porter 2002a: 51). Alternative medicine is gaining a degree of legitimacy denied it for much of the twentieth century, and this is based in part on the rise of a more consumerist outlook on the part of prospective patients (Cant and Sharma 1999). The rise of 'non-clinician physicians' in the USA (McKinlay and Marceau 2002: Cooper and Stoflet 2004) and the expansion of medical markets in many countries (as lay people seek help for an ever wider range of health-related problems) create structural changes in health care which add to the decline in medical dominance and an unchallenged medical autonomy. Nurses and other practitioners such as community pharmacists are exercising more autonomy and practising more directly with patients, outside direct medical control (Bury 2004). The patient may not be the new ruler, but a more informed patient-oriented approach to health care consumption is coinciding with a more pluralistic form of health care provision.

Changes in health policy

Finally, we need to take note of changes in the political and policy arenas, as they influence health care, some of which have been alluded to in the above discussion. While these form part of the 'external' context governing health care, their importance suggests that they should be considered in their own right as well. Many of the particular issues discussed so far – for example, the decline in the autonomy of medical practitioners and the pressure to develop a 'partnership' approach with patients – are now finding their way into formal policy initiatives, both in the USA and in the UK. All have implications for changing social relations in health care.

The first issue concerns the relationship between managers, doctors and patients. In the UK, governments have recently embarked on a 'modernization' agenda, aimed, it is argued, at ensuring that the NHS is more responsive to patients' needs and offers value for money. In the late 1990s the Labour Government of the time set out a range of targets concerning the delivery of health care, especially in the area of waiting times for surgery. Managers in the NHS were held to account for failures to meet such targets, and this led to considerable pressure being placed on doctors to set aside their clinical judgement about who might be most in need, in favour of meeting their set targets. Clashes between managers and doctors revolved round constraints on the latter to exercise clinical autonomy. Seeing or treating an individual patient within the time limit set by the target might involve delaying a clinically more urgent case. However, it became clear in the ensuing years that waiting time targets were not likely to be reduced dramatically by the policy, and they were quietly side-lined. The NHS Plan launched in the year 2000, together with National Service Frameworks, the Wanless Reports and the NHS Improvement Plan which followed, have tended instead to emphasize broader issues of improving quality, choice and standards of care. The legacy of poor relationships between managers and doctors over targets, however, has been less easy to deal with. At the time of writing (June 2004) the UK government is claiming that many of the earlier targets for reducing waiting times are now being met.

Of equal importance in dealing with issues concerning cost, clinical autonomy and the evaluation of treatment in medical practice (especially evidence derived from RCTs) is the work of new organizations such as the National Institute of Clinical Excellence (NICE) established in 1999. The stated aim of this particular body is 'to provide patients, health care professionals and the public with authoritative, robust and reliable guidance on "best practice"' (<www.nice.org.uk>). From the outset, NICE was liable to court controversy, if only because its pronouncements on 'best practice' were likely to clash with a range of interests in health care, not least of which were those of patients. In particular, as Fitzpatrick has noted, 'considerable controversy has been aroused by decisions not to recommend public funding for interventions for which evaluative research provides insufficient evidence of effectiveness' (Fitzpatrick 2004: 248).

Although the chairman of NICE has stated that cost effectiveness is not the 'sole criterion' for judging the value of a treatment (Rawlins 2001), this is clearly a defensive response to critics who have argued that NICE is, essentially, a government tool for effecting rationing in the NHS (Smith 2000). A number of test cases have been at the centre of the controversy over the role of NICE – notably its decision in 2001 not to fund the use of beta interferon in the treatment of multiple sclerosis. Although this was couched in terms of the lack of evidence of effectiveness, manufacturers of the drug, together with individual doctors and patient groups, rejected the recommendation and called on the government to overrule it. The government, in fact, went on to do so, calling for evidence to be collected from individual patient experiences of the drug (Mayor 2001). Whilst this policy move clashed with the emphasis on trial-level evidence, it expressed all too clearly the tensions between a patient-oriented health care system and the pressure to evaluate treatment and promote 'evidence-based' practice.

In the USA, policies to control costs and to constrain clinical autonomy have taken a somewhat different route – that of 'managed care'. As Wholey and Burns (2000: 217) have argued, the development of Managed Care Organizations (MCOs) represents a policy shift within a market-based system towards emphasizing that quality measurement, guidelines and risk adjustment are necessary for controlling expanding health care activities. Unlike bodies such as NICE in the UK, MCOs are 'not accountable for producing research as a public good' (Wholey and Burns 2000: 219). Rather, they support research that improves quality at a certain cost, depending on the particular treatment module in question. It is also the case that MCOs are not designed to deliver health care to uninsured populations, and manage care only for particular population groups. Thus they are not a route for the socialization of health care in line with European practice. They are, however, according to Wholey and Burns, a sign that the USA system is being transformed from one dominated by the medical profession to one characterized by market and bureaucratic mechanisms. Their development has been effective in controlling costs, though this may have been at a price of disrupting existing relationships between patients and their doctors (p. 232). The 'corporatization' of American health care, and the end of the 'golden age of medicine', has its social costs as well as its financial savings (McKinlay and Marceau 2002). Examples such as that of Kaiser Permanente in California suggest, however, that corporate and medical interests may be combined (Ham et al. 2003).

Returning to the broad policy context, a final comment should be added concerning initiatives aimed more directly at patients in the health care system. Mention has already been made of ideas such as 'partnership' and 'shared care' in the UK NHS. Of all the policy initiatives taken in this area, perhaps that of the 'Expert Patient' is the most emblematic of change in UK health care. This initiative, set in train by the government's Chief Medical Officer (CMO), Liam Donaldson, became part of the ten-year 'NHS Plan' put in place in the year 2000. The ideas behind the initiative reflect, again, moves away from medical paternalism, and a recognition that lay people and patients are active agents in health maintenance and care. In particular, the Expert Patient Programme (EPP) builds on the insight that, in the case of chronic illnesses at least, patients may have as much, if not more, knowledge about their condition as their doctors. Donaldson argues that the 'wisdom and experience of the patient has been only a tacit form of knowledge whose potential to improve the outcome of care and quality of life has been largely untapped' (Donaldson 2003: 1279).

The EPP in the UK is based on the work of Kate Lorig and her co-workers at Stanford University. By training 'lay leaders' in a 'chronic disease self-management programme' (CDSMP), Lorig showed that patients with arthritis and other disorders who were offered a carefully scripted course had better outcomes in terms of self-rated health, disability and everyday performance of roles in comparison with those receiving standard treatment (Lorig et al. 1999). As a result of this evidence and a desire to emphasize a patient-centred approach to health policy, the CMO's initiative is being implemented (now as part of the UK government's Modernization Agency) on a pilot basis in 100 primary care services in England, during the period 2004–7. Linked with the idea of partnership, the CMO has advocated the EPP as heralding a 'new era of optimism and opportunity' in health care for the chronically ill (Donaldson 2003: 1280). Here, health providers may become distant 'partners', with 'lay experts' empowering other patients. Thus the relationship between health and health care turns full circle, with patients appearing at the centre of a modernization agenda, with their own degree of 'autonomy' (Coulter 2002).

At the official level, then, we hear perhaps an echo of Frank's notion of patients 'recolonizing' illness – though the acceptability of the Expert Patient Programme, to patients and practitioners alike, is less than clear (Wilson 2001; Kennedy at al. 2004). Patients may often want doctors to do what they are paid to do, and act in the patient's best interest, especially when illness is serious and difficult to manage. In addition, legal responsibilities for treatment and care are not easily transferred from the doctor to the patient. It is too early, therefore, to tell whether this initiative will be effective or not, despite the fact that its advent is creating considerable interest inside and outside policy circles. To use a well-worn phrase, it is worth 'watching this space'.

Concluding Remark

The sentiments expressed above by the CMO about the 'Expert Patient' are a far cry from earlier views of the medical profession in which the doctor knew best and the patient was by definition ignorant. It is possible, of course, to see such initiatives as attempts to reduce costs by making patients less reliant on the health service, or as further limits on medical autonomy. Many such initiatives will no doubt also prove to be largely the passing rhetoric of a professional elite, or attempts at 'top-down' paternalistic policies, albeit in benign and apparently 'empowering' forms. Some may bring definite improvements in health care. However, their sociological significance also lies in the fact that the medical profession is seeking to renegotiate its legitimacy in the health care field, and is coming to terms with the dynamic of health politics and changes in the social relations of health care now under way. Not all professionals or patients will respond positively to such moves, whether in terms of 'partnership' or in terms of patient autonomy and 'self-management'. But the changes that are afoot in professional–patient relationships, alongside the evaluation of treatments – in population or individual terms – and the greater accountability of doctors, set the scene for a new agenda for health care practice, and thus for sociological research.

6

The Future of Health
and Illness

Introduction

The eminent British historian Sir Michael Howard has made the point that peace is much more than the absence of war (Howard 2002: 2). A similar case can be argued with respect to health: as noted at the outset, it is clearly much more than the absence of disease. This 'Short Introduction' has sought to show that health is a dynamic process: it changes across the lifecourse, and it differs depending on historical and social circumstances. Such processes will obviously influence exposure to particular health risks and the experience of illness, including the use and outcomes of health care. Someone born in the UK or the USA in 2005 will not experience the same health risks as someone born in those societies in 1905 or even 1955. To be born into a less developed society, even today, carries with it risks to health (for example, from infectious illnesses) rarely experienced in the West. Periods of economic decline, political upheaval and war can cut across the health of individuals and the public in any society. Lay definitions and perceptions of health also change, even in periods of relative stability, as do the scientific and professional 'framing' of disease and illness.

It is important to recognize the complex nature of health and illness, if only to avoid their reduction to one dimension (for example, their biological or genetic basis), but complexity itself is a source of potential frustration. The tendency for academic debate to stress complexity can annoy those who look for practical solutions to real-life problems, whether health practitioners or policy-makers. The inequalities debate in health is an obvious case in point. As chapter 2 has shown, a very large research endeavour is now under way, and on an international scale, to improve understanding of health inequalities. Studies of social class, ethnicity, gender, age, the lifecourse and (geographical) place are just some of the topics receiving current and growing attention. The inequalities revealed are often real and important. Yet, few if any studies give any clear indication, in practical or political terms, of what might be done to reduce them. To show that income inequality is linked with health, for example, does not address the thorny political issue of income redistribution, of how it might be achieved in different societies, or with what consequences. Policy thinking, arguably, trails far behind scientific research. Few attempts have been made to redress this imbalance by exploring how positive policies might have an impact on reducing health inequalities (see exceptions such as Whitehead et al. 2000; Mackenbach and Bakker 2003). Those policies that exist to promote the population's health can also, paradoxically, have negative social consequences, and need careful evaluation. It is certainly the case that some policies have led to *increases* in inequalities: smoking today has a strong inverse relationship with social class, partly as the result of anti-smoking messages being taken up selectively by the better-off. Obesity and changes in diet show similar patterns. Many recommendations for health-related behaviours are adopted by those least at risk.

In some ways, it is understandable, therefore, that prescriptions for change are reluctantly given and hard to come by. Some researchers take the view that it is their job to provide the evidence and that of others to decide on policy. More generally, there is a reluctance to offer simple solutions to the complex problems that go to make up many of the health issues in contemporary societies. Unintended consequences of policy prescriptions can offset original intentions. Moreover, the rapidity of cultural and (bio) technical change is so great as to make suggestions for tackling them seem out of date before the ink is dry. A sociological view of health and its future is perhaps best served by attempting to 'figure out what is going on', rather than trying to tell others what actions they should take, though the implications for 'real world' problems can sometimes be spelled out.

This chapter concludes our discussion of health and illness, therefore, by trying to discern some of the main features of the present that are likely to influence the future – at least, those in developed societies such as the USA and the UK. The chapter first outlines key developments in the social context of health and illness in contemporary societies, including the blurring of boundaries, the extension of medicalization and medical surveillance. The chapter then goes on to consider critically some of the ways in which these can be most fruitfully understood from a sociological viewpoint. It is hoped that by this route a picture of the future will emerge.

Health in a Late Modern Context

Perhaps one of the most definable features of health in contemporary society is its subjective character. Today, in sharp contrast with even a few years ago, official thinking in medical and policy circles is stressing the lay or patient viewpoint. This shift in official discourse results from, and adds to, general changes in social relations. As a result of consumerism and changes in market economies, together with a growing 'populism' and 'informalism' in the surrounding culture, areas of experience that were once hidden from view, or managed by 'objectifying' experts such as doctors, have taken on greater social salience. A focus on the subjective involves playing down the 'grand narratives' of science and technology, or at least putting their authority in recurrent doubt. In turn, these processes raise the profile of lay or patient narratives (Bury 1998, 2001). Developments such as lifecourse research also serve to reinforce 'biographical' processes in health, and thus the importance of personal experience as much as objective 'health status'. Indeed, at times, health in its subjective dimensions seems to be the *leitmotif* of contemporary culture.

These developments in health and illness seem to be here to stay, and many organizations are trying to face up to their implications. The health care professions are particularly in the firing line. As Coulter and Fitzpatrick (2000) argue, health care professionals are now being educated and trained to communicate more effectively with patients and to take their level of satisfaction with the process and outcome of care more seriously. As we saw in chapter 5, initiatives to promote shared decision making and 'patient partnership' are now firmly on the agenda of health services in countries such as the UK. Until recently it was widely held that lay people and patients could (and should) know very little about the content of their care; today all manner of information can be accessed about disease and its treatment, as well the management of symptoms in everyday life. Coulter and Fitzpatrick make the point that whilst in the past the patient's viewpoint was seen as a threat to professional autonomy, today there is a 'substantial momentum' behind making health services more responsive in this regard (p. 462). Professionals will need, in the future, to incorporate the patient's view into their practice in a number of different ways, ranging from informed consent to greater participation in health care planning. This pressure is likely to continue and increase in the future.

Having said this, it is also clear that arguments that we live in an increasingly 'contestable' as well as 'reflexive' culture are particularly relevant to the future for health and health care. For, while the patient or lay view is being emphasized in policy or research circles, the potential for *conflict* between subjective experience and medical authority has received less attention. Yet many examples exist where lay and medical views of health and health care diverge, and where 'partnership' is less evident. This is especially true, perhaps, where views about health and illness go beyond personal experience in the clinic, and begin to engage with wider public health matters. Such disputes are likely to increase in the future. A recent example from the UK can illustrate the point being made here.

In February 1998 an 'early report' by a team of 13 authors from a North London Hospital (Wakefield et al. 1998) appeared in the medical journal *The Lancet* which suggested (on the basis of a study of a small number of patients) that autism might be linked to gastrointestinal disease, and possibly to the combined vaccine for measles, mumps and rubella (MMR). Although the report clearly stated that the link with the MMR vaccine was not proven, it listed all of the 12 cases under review, showing that the children's doctors and/or parents had linked the onset of autism in time to MMR vaccination – with onset often being seen within 24 or 48 hours. Despite its caution about causal influences, the report clearly expressed concern about the triple vaccine. Although one of the leading authors went on to support the continued use of the MMR vaccine (writing to *The Lancet* in May 1998 to say so), the original report, and a press conference on the subject, led to considerable public reaction. This showed little sign of waning with the passage of time. Parents began to campaign around the demand that their children be offered separate vaccinations for the three diseases, pending further enquiry into the side effects of the triple jab, especially its links with autism, and with childhood bowel disease. These strongly expressed lay views began to appear regularly in the press and in other media.

However, far from accepting the lay viewpoint and agreeing to separate vaccinations, the British government and Department of Health mounted a counter campaign to stem the flow of parental and media-led demand. As Richard Smith, editor of the *British Medical Journal*, noted in a later editorial on 'The discomfort of patient power' (Smith 2002), the government marshalled a considerable body of evidence to show that the MMR vaccine was safe, and that it would be 'folly to offer parents the choice of having their children vaccinated separately against each disease' (p. 497). The government's Chief Medical Officer, Sir Liam Donaldson, appeared frequently on British television and radio in an attempt to reassure parents that medical opinion and research overwhelmingly supported the use of the triple MMR vaccine. In the end, the government had its way, and while some doctors provided separate vaccines privately, the official position held firm, and parental choice in the NHS was denied. As Smith points out in his editorial, although the government had been stressing the patient view, patient partnership and choice in recent policy initiatives, this clearly could not encompass the prospect of patients making 'wrong' or 'foolish' decisions – even though telling individual parents this in the clinic setting would be difficult indeed.

Whatever the rights and wrongs of this particular case (in November 2003 two of the leading authors of the initial report themselves added a further twist to the story by entering into public conflict about the vaccine, and in February 2004 allegations of a conflict of interest were made against the lead author of the original paper), it expressed clearly many of the contours of the 'contestable culture' noted above. The publication of a single report of possible negative effects of immunization, backed up by a dramatic press conference, led to widespread public concern if not panic. The ensuing conflict between parents and medical opinion revealed that the rhetoric about subjective experience and the patient view could only go so far before it clashed with the authority of leading members of the medical profession and more 'objective' (though contested) scientific evidence about the working of the body and medical treatment. The case has not been without its legal dimensions either, with families involved in a complex lawsuit against three drug companies. This shows little sign of resolution (*The Guardian*, 12 May 2004). Behind this example, then, a number of important processes influencing the shape of health and health care in late modern society have been evident. The rest of this section goes on to spell out in a little more detail what some of these are.

The blurring of boundaries

The case of the MMR vaccine turned in part on the use of a treatment to prevent illness in otherwise healthy individuals. At the time of vaccination, it is the *future* health status of the individual that is being considered, not their current health state. As such, it is not a 'treatment' for illness, but a technique that manipulates the body's mechanisms in order, hopefully, to forestall future health risks for the individual and the wider community. This is not a new situation, of course, as vaccination has existed in Western societies for many generations. However, in a populist culture such as that obtaining today, the contradiction of intervention in an otherwise healthy individual becomes more open to question. This is especially the case, perhaps, in a period where many diseases seem to have lost their capacity to cause fear, and where medical research is routinely questioned as to its truthfulness. At the same time, whilst scepticism about medical intervention abounds, many individuals engage in medical treatments for a wide range of reasons that often have only an indirect relationship to disease or illness.

This blurring of boundaries surrounding health, then, is not confined to the dynamics of preventive medicine. What counts as 'normal' versus 'pathological' is now far more open to question, as is the role of medical treatment. Illness as a form of deviance (whether biological or social) becomes problematic, as does the notion of 'deviance' itself. Again, the decline in mortality from infectious diseases plays a part here. As was seen earlier in this book, the authority of the 'medical model' of health and illness was based on a pathological and anatomical view of disease, where specific causes (a bacterium or virus) could be linked with specific disease outcomes. However, much of what preoccupies both lay and medical thought today sits uneasily within such a model, especially as technological developments have grown apace. Medical treatment, as well as preventive action, is often undertaken today under conditions where pathology is absent. Just two examples from many will serve as illustrations of this wider set of problems.

The first, as noted in chapter 4, is what can be called medical or bodily 'enhancement' – that is, where medical interventions are aimed not at curing disease, or indeed treating illness at all, but at altering a feature of the person's body, mind or performance. In a recent discussion of the subject, Conrad and Jacobson (2003) consider the example of the rapid growth and popularity of breast augmentation. They estimate that in the United States, from the 1960s to the 1990s, some 2 million women received silicone implants, 80 per cent of whom did so for cosmetic rather than disease (cancer)-related reasons (p. 228). During the 1990s concerns about potential risks to women's health from silicone implants began to surface, as did allegations of a lack of information about safety from the manufacturers. This led to restrictions on their use, and a rise in use of saline implants, which, though lined with silicone, are filled with water. The decline in the use of the old implants was soon compensated by strong demand by women for the new, saline implants. In 2000 alone there were more than 203,000 such implants in the USA (p. 229).

Such developments pose sharp questions about the role of medicine in providing treatments for what might be seen as non-medical problems. The commercial and ethical issues involved in medical interventions of this kind are matters of concern. But the blurring of the boundary between medical and social or psychological needs challenges both ethical and social thought. It is possible to argue, of course, that the demand for breast enhancement reflects dominant cultural motifs governing what is taken to be an acceptable body image. Both male domination and medical collusion can be charged with perpetuating such imagery, and indeed profiting from it. Yet, as Conrad and Jacobson point out, despite the influence of 'media norms', women negotiate their way around a complex cultural terrain and actively participate in the 'cosmetic surgery decision-making process' (p. 230). No simple prescription can be offered here. In a consumer-led (medical) culture, demand for goods and services is created through interactions between customers and producers. Many areas of health are affected by such processes.

A similar set of complex issues surrounds the second example to be considered: namely, infertility and assisted reproduction treatment (ART). Ever since the inception of in vitro fertilization and the first 'test tube' baby born in Britain in 1982, the issue of 'treatment' for infertility has been a controversial issue. There are many reasons for this, including arguments concerning the creation, storage and use of human embryos, their ownership, and potential for medical research. Today, for example, it is not possible for Federal funds in the USA to be used for 'stem cell' research using embryos, whereas this is allowed on a limited basis in the UK (Parens and Knowles 2003). Similarly, in some countries and regions (for example, Finland, Western Australia) it is mandatory for parents seeking ART to give consent for the results of 'treatment' (whether a baby is born and survives or not, and the long-term health of any baby born) to be followed up and investigated by approved researchers. In many other countries it is not. Reported risks of new forms of ART (Hansen et al. 2002) are hotly debated. In addition, the provision of ART in many countries is largely through privately run clinics (even where there are socialized health care systems, as in the UK and Finland), and this has allowed considerable financial interests and market forces to flourish. The regulation and evaluation of the rapidly developing technologies in this field struggle to keep up with the dynamics and complexities involved, whether they be scientific, financial, ethical or social.

For present purposes, it is the blurring of the boundary between health and illness that is of note in here. Whether infertility should be regarded as a medical problem, or a 'disease', is clearly open to question. One or other parent involved in ART may suffer from a reproductive disorder, but this is not the same as saying that they are ill. This helps to explain the reluctance of many countries to fund such treatment publicly. The 'opportunity costs' of funding infertility treatment – that is, the effects of any such funding on the ability to provide other health services – may be considerable, particularly as most of the individual treatment cycles fail, and parents may seek to repeat the process on a number of occasions. Not only that, if the risks of ART turn out to be high, for the children or their mothers, the impact on health services, as well as on the lives of those directly affected, may be considerable. The desire to have children may be seen variously as 'natural' or 'socially constructed', but attempts to remedy infertility raise a host of issues that cut across any simple categorization.

Indeed, the situation is even more complex when genetics meets reproductive technology – what Parens and Knowles (2003) term 'reprogenetics'. Although the branches of medical science dealing with genetics and reproduction have developed in separate ways, and under different forms of regulation and 'governance', they are now meeting in the areas of embryonic research, gene transfer, cloning and gene therapy. The blurring of this particular divide also connects with the question of enhancement and choice of bodily characteristics. Parens and Knowles note, for example, that some 430 children have been born in the USA as the result of sex selection. The ability to choose the sex of a baby, with an 85 per cent accuracy, relies on the ability to sort sperm in terms of the weight of the chromosomes they carry (p. 4). Sex selection has thus become a technical possibility far in advance of any clarity about the social values involved.

In addition, considerable controversy has surrounded the selection of embryos for traits other than sex, such as in the case of Jamie Whitaker in the UK. Jamie was born in 2003, having been 'selected' in the hope that he would serve as a match for his 4-year-old brother, Charlie, who suffers from a rare form of anaemia. The procedure which allowed for the selection to take place is legal in the USA but not in the UK. The parents therefore travelled to the USA in order for this to take place. Now that it has been shown that the match is good, stem cells can be used from Jamie's umbilical cord to treat Charlie (BBC news report, 2 November 2003). Although in this case the parents were adamant that Jamie was a wanted baby irrespective of his 'matching' capability, arguments about 'designer babies', and the selection of traits, whether for clinical or other reasons, continue, further eroding the boundaries between medicine, health and social processes. Frank's (1995) idea of the remission society, where the majority if not most of the population suffer from or have (partially) recovered from a health disorder, takes on even greater salience under conditions of rapidly changing bio-technology and medical 'treatment'. We may all be disordered or recovering in the future, and thus candidates for one form of treatment or another.

The extension of medicalization

The developments described above can be seen, perhaps, to constitute a further extension of the 'medicalization of society' – long argued over, inside and outside sociological circles. There are many examples of new forms of medicalization that can be given, in addition to those of enhancement, fertility and human reproduction. Space permits mention of only two or three, to illustrate some of the issues likely to shape the future of health. The first of these concerns wider areas of child health and child behaviour. The extension of medical treatment to more and more aspects of children's lives and health has grown considerably in recent years. Perhaps the most dramatic example has been the rise of the use of methylphenidate (Ritalin, a drug related to amphetamine) for the treatment of 'attention deficit hyperactivity disorder' (ADHD), though other drugs are also now in use. In 1998 the National Institutes for Health in the USA set up an expert panel to advise on the diagnosis and treatment of ADHD, and although it reported that 'our knowledge about the cause or causes of ADHD remains speculative', and that there were no strategies for prevention, it also reported that some 3–5 per cent of school-age children were affected by ADHD in the USA, and that about 3 per cent took Ritalin (Charatan 1998).

In the UK, in 2000, and then with an update in 2003, the National Institute for Clinical Excellence (NICE) issued guidance on the use of medicines for treating ADHD. In its first appraisal it estimated that 1 per cent of children aged 6–16 in England and Wales were seriously affected, amounting to some 69,000 young people, with an overall prevalence of 5 per cent – that is, more than 350,000 children. It was estimated that 25,000 were receiving Ritalin (NICE 2000). The NICE guidelines make it clear that Ritalin is not licensed in the UK for children under 6, and that when it is used, it should be part of a 'comprehensive treatment programme' and involve regular monitoring. Although the advice is couched in measured terms, the fact that NICE, like the US expert panel, convened to consider the use of Ritalin suggests at least some cause for concern. Whilst it is possible to argue that 'disorders' such as ADHD may have been hidden from view in the past, and are now recognized partly because of an available treatment, it is equally arguable that the advent of the drug has helped to create the disorders it seeks to treat. Child health thus becomes a potentially huge market for medicaments, and a site for transforming developmental difficulties or problematic behaviours (and their management by parents and teachers alike) into medical issues. Recent press reports about the extension of the use of anti-depressants involving an estimated 50,000 children in the UK (*The Guardian*, 20 September 2003) have added to the growing controversy about child health.

Similar fears about the extension of medicalization have been raised with respect to the other end of the lifecourse – that is, to the relationship between health and medicine in old age. In the UK, at least, as Ebrahim (2002) has noted, historically, medical care was extended to older people in the NHS through the development of geriatric medicine. In fact, geriatrics was part of a reconceptualization of old age in which degeneration and senescence became the focus of biological and clinical thought (Katz 1996). Growing older was increasingly seen as problematic, and although geriatric medicine offered care for the sick elderly (offsetting a tendency in the British NHS to ration care by age, and exclude the elderly), it was, to some extent at least, at the cost of neglecting positive health and vitality in old age. 'Normal ageing' itself became transformed into a disease, with the idea that the passage of time would necessarily mean the loss of function and biological capacity. A new boundary was drawn around old age, conceptualizing many of the processes involved as pathological.

Today, however, successive cohorts of people who are healthier in their early and middle years may bring with them the prospect of a healthier lifestyle in old age, and a possible reduction in medicalization, as poor health and disability are confined to the very last years of life. There is not space here to discuss fully the debate surrounding these developments (Bury 2000), but it is certainly the case that geriatric health care has been declining in the UK as patients have been moved from hospitals to nursing homes, and a greater emphasis has been placed on social care. Commentators in both the UK and the USA have queried the wisdom of carrying out expensive and invasive medical treatment, especially in the very old, whose life expectancy is clearly less than that of younger patients. 'Demedicalization' of old age seems to be a real possibility.

However, the potential for the extension of medical treatments *in* old age, as opposed to the treatment of old age as a medical problem, opens up new avenues for medicalization. As the population of more affluent, healthy and less deferential older people grows, expectations and demands for medical treatment may, somewhat paradoxically, rise. The increasing ability of medical treatments and technologies to be used successfully in old age will undoubtedly fuel this process. An otherwise healthy older individual may be able to withstand invasive treatment for a specific medical condition much better than a similarly aged person in the past, and this may already be leading to the growth of medical markets in later life. Healthier older people may demand more acute medical care, including more forms of surgery. Arguments about the negative aspects of medicalization in later life – risks of infections in hospitals, over-prescribing, and especially the consumption of drugs such as tranquillizers and hypnotics (sleeping pills) in later life – are balanced against the desirable features of good-quality medical care, including high-tech procedures, being made available to people of all ages (Ebrahim 2002). Thus demedicalization and remedicalization can occur at the same time.

The final example to be discussed here briefly is that of obesity. As chapters 2 and 4 have shown, the medical implications of obesity across the life-course are attracting growing attention. Indeed, the current tendency to discuss obesity as an 'epidemic' suggests a level of public and health care concern bordering on panic. The medical correlates of obesity are not difficult to see, especially its association with diabetes and raised blood pressure (Bury and Wadsworth 2003). Increases in both obesity and diabetes among children are particularly worrying from a public health point of view. It is of interest to note that such concern is in marked contrast to fears about child health and under-nutrition in other periods of history, and in other cultures today. In the past obesity among adults was taken as a sign of overindulgence among a minority of the well-to-do; today, though common, it is increasingly a sign of social deprivation.

As Chang and Christakis (2002) have noted, estimates suggest that in the USA up to half the population may now be overweight or obese. In the UK similarly rapid rises in obesity have been observed, with rates tripling in the last 20 years and fast approaching US levels (p. 152). Chang and Christakis go on to argue that the trend towards medicalizing obesity has been equally noticeable, with powerful medical claims to control fatness, 'ranging from defining it as a disease to the application of a wide range of medical treatments' (p. 152). They go on to show that in medical textbooks, at least, there has been a significant change over time in the presentation of obesity, from an emphasis on an excess of calorie intake to the body, to one emphasizing the patient's experience. Here, again, the subjectivity of the patient is given increasing attention in official medical thought.

The point being made in Chang and Christakis's analysis is that medicalizing a problem such as obesity can lead to its transformation from a moral or social issue into a medical or technical one, and this sets up an important tension. On the one hand, medicalizing obesity can lead to a reduction in the stigma and moral opprobrium attached to it. To this extent it may be welcomed as much by the layperson as by the medical scientist or practitioner. On the other hand, medicalization can lead to the disguising or avoidance of the moral or political issues that underpin the problem. An emphasis on possible biological or genetic predispositions to obesity, for example, underpins claims that the condition is 'natural' and in need of medical treatment. In this way the moral and social issues surrounding over-eating and lack of exercise – issues of agency recognized by Chang and Christakis – are ignored, as are the political issues connected with the production and promotion of cheap and plentiful foods by supermarkets and restaurants (Chou et al. 2004). At the very least, in terms of the discussion of health offered throughout this book, the extension of medicalization, alongside the blurring of boundaries, reinforces the tendency to see a health-related issue such as obesity as a relational and social phenomenon rather than simply an attribute of the individual.

Surveillance and health

The future of health is also likely to involve increasing levels of surveillance over the individual, from birth (indeed, before birth *in utero*) to the last years of life. The tendency for surveillance to increase in modern societies has been noted by a number of sociologists, alongside the contestable and reflexive features of contemporary cultures mentioned earlier (Giddens 1991). Increases in surveillance arise, in general, as a result of attempts to administer complex societies under conditions of uncertainty, and where direct political control of individuals is relatively weak. Attempts to monitor the views and behaviours of citizens also arise when social cohesion and regulation is fragile – witness the growth of the use of CCTV cameras in the case of crime and accident prevention. Much surveillance concerns the body, or rather bodies, moving around in social spaces where they might pose particular threats to social order – in football stadiums, shopping malls or city centre precincts. Self-surveillance is important, too, though problematical, as individuals are encouraged to exercise self-restraint and at the same time regard the body as a site for extensive consumerism and self-expression.

These cultural strains are reflected in and contributed to by medical surveillance, whether 'objectively' via the expansion of medical technologies or 'subjectively' through the adoption of healthy lifestyles and the need to monitor bodily systems for early signs of disorder. The 'surveillance society' (Blaxter 2004) involves monitoring self and others for the 'probabilities of ill health' in the future (p. 89). The rapid growth of scientific and technical knowledge of the body promises to bring considerable benefits to individuals through improved medical procedures, better prediction and more effective treatments. At the same time it gives cause for concern as the side effects or unintended consequences of such developments are envisaged or become apparent.

There are many examples that could be considered here. Perhaps the most important, and the one that is likely to have the most far-reaching effects on health in the future, concerns the 'new genetics'. As was seen above in the case of 'reprogenetics', the growth of activity in the field of genetic science shows no signs of slowing. Even though genetic inheritance probably contributes between 1 and 5 per cent to the disease burden of society (Blaxter 2003: 74), the completion of the Human Genome Project, which finally mapped the human genome in 2001, has many implications for health and the surveillance of individuals. In addition to disorders with direct genetic causes, such as Huntington's disease or Duchenne muscular dystrophy, many others are being investigated in terms of the 'gene/environment' interactions that might help to explain them more adequately (Pilnick 2002). Populations and individuals (many of whom, at the point of contact, may be healthy) can be studied in order to uncover the interactions involved here. Large-scale data gathering is already under way, or planned, in many countries, in order to study them more fully.

In the UK, for example, a new study called 'Biobank', based at the University of Manchester, is carrying out a major project from 2005 onwards, in which up to half a million participants between the ages of 45 and 69 years of age will give a blood sample, and provide lifestyle details and their medical histories to 'create a national database of unprecedented size' (<www.biobank.ac.uk>, accessed 14 November 2003). The Chief Executive Officer for the project is quoted as saying that, 'following the Human Genome Project, the new genetics provides a stunning opportunity to move ahead in our understanding of variability in human health . . . the UK Biobank will allow the risk of disease to be predicted in populations. Predicting risk in individuals is not the aim of the study.' None the less, a detailed ethical framework has been developed by 'Biobank' in order for the information to be gathered from individuals, and for it to be made available to academic researchers and those in pharmaceutical companies attempting to develop new and effective treatments. Insurance companies may not access the information gathered, though, and it may take up to 30 years for the results of the study to show their 'true value'.

Gathering genetic information for individual medical management is, however, receiving attention in other initiatives. Such is the assumed potential of the techniques involved that genetic technology is expanding rapidly in both the private and the public sectors. In the UK, between 2003 and 2006, £50 million of government money is being provided to upgrade NHS genetic laboratories, and to develop services in primary care and in hospitals. The aim here is to expand the range of tests that individuals can be given which might tell them that they are at risk from a particular disorder – so-called predictive genetics. Measures to help prevent or treat any disorder discovered could then be put in place at an earlier stage than would otherwise be the case. Indeed, consideration is being given to the idea of screening babies at birth and storing their genetic profiles for use in the future. These developments are part of major discussions about the future of genetics in the UK, such as that in the White Paper 'Our Inheritance Our Future: Realising the Potential of Genetics in the NHS' (Cmnd 5971, June 2003). A new Human Genetics Commission is charged with considering the many social and ethical issues that flow from such developments.

All of these developments have the potential for bringing about many gains for individuals and for society as a whole, in terms of its public health. But disquiet about the surveillance of the populations and individuals involved has been frequently expressed. Causes of disquiet range from the doubtful ethics of knowing about possible future states of health from predictive testing, to the dangers of becoming uninsurable or more generally discriminated against as a member of a 'genetic underclass'. This might take the form, for example, of being barred from working in a particular job because of a genetic risk to a particular hazard (Dingwall 2002: 177). And, of course, the emphasis on identifying 'abnormalities', especially at birth, gives rise to fears of a recurrence of a form of eugenics where only the fit and healthy are valued. Debates in the field of disability studies have raised questions not only about such matters as prenatal screening, but also about the ability of genetics to 'reconfigure our knowledge about disability in ways that will impact on non-disabled people, as well as on disabled people' (Shakespeare 2003: 208). As with the examples of 'blurring' given above, what counts as being disabled or being healthy may become more difficult to resolve in the future.

Finally, as Conrad (2000) has pointed out, the weight given to genetic explanations in public discourse, as much as in medical, commercial or governmental circles, runs the risk of implying that 'genes are *the* main cause of a problem' (p. 325, emphasis in the original). In contrast to social-scientific or epidemiological explanations of health, which often, as we have noted, stress complexity rather than direct cause and effect, genetics seems to offer a compelling if somewhat mystical story about the essence of our bodies and our health. Whilst many scientists in the field of genetics point to the complex interactions between genes and environment, as in the example of 'Biobank' above, public discussion and media coverage frequently portray genes as a 'privileged cause', deflecting attention from other factors influencing health. As genetic science identifies an ever increasing number of traits, including possibly behavioural ones, the extension of surveillance of individuals and populations through the 'new genetics' will reach into the future of health in ways that can be seen only dimly at present. The 'biomedicalization' of health suggests that 'everyone is potentially ill', and that in the future it will be 'impossible not to be at risk' (Clarke et al. 2003: 172–3).

Understanding Health and Illness in the Future

The final question to be addressed in this 'Short Introduction', and following on from the above, is: how can the future of health and illness be best understood from a sociological point of view? One response to the changing pattern of health exemplified by the kind of processes outlined above – the blurring of boundaries, the extension of medicalization, and increasing surveillance – is to argue that a 'postmodern' culture has emerged where the development of medical science and technology meets preoccupations with subjectivity and the body (Bury 1998). Here, the problem is a concern not so much with 'medicalization' as with what Robert Crawford, over 20 years ago, called 'healthism' (Crawford 1980). In a culture which explains 'life chances' and 'well-being' in strongly individualistic terms, health consciousness and health-related social movements – including those, according to Crawford, that emphasize holistic health care and self-care – take on particular salience. As has been noted earlier in this book, no matter how much health has improved objectively (lower mortality, longer life expectancy, better health care and cleaner, safer environments), the reporting of health problems continues to grow, rather than diminish. Moreover, markets for health, both orthodox and complementary, seem to become ever larger, simultaneously meeting and exploiting expressed need.

Equally, there is no shortage of critiques or critics of the processes at work. There are a number of possible perspectives that can be drawn upon in medical sociology. Echoing the writings of Illich in the 1970s, Shorter (1993), for example, has pointed to the tendency of people in contemporary societies to emphasize bodily ailments such as pain and fatigue. Although there is nothing in principle new in this, Shorter argues that today lay people are 'more sensitive generally to the signals their bodies give off, and they are more ready to assign these symptoms to a given "attribution" – a fixed diagnosis of organic disease' (Shorter 1993: 295). This 'attributional' view of health can be seen in public discussions of a wide range of disorders: ADHD resulting from a faulty brain, ME/CFS caused by a viral infection, or obesity caused by a faulty gene. Many other conditions which have hitherto evaded an organic or 'attributional' location are being drawn into the net, perhaps the most dramatic being depression, which is widely believed to be caused by the lack of serotonin in the brain (Healy 1999).

Shorter's analysis of the tendency for lay people increasingly to attribute their bodily and psychological discomforts to illness with an organic basis suggests that social forces are partly responsible. Shorter notes, in particular, what he sees as a 'distinctively "postmodern" disaffiliation from family life' (p. 295), and a tendency for the media and 'self-help' groups to amplify lay people's concerns. As far as the link with family life is concerned, Shorter argues that rising divorce rates and other changes in family structure give rise to instability and 'an increase in solitude' (p. 321). People are more likely to live alone, or in two-person households (Abercrombie 2004: 28). One-parent families have risen rapidly in the last 20 years. In such circumstances people are less likely to be able to test out their feelings or bodily signals within a supportive (and controlling) intimate relationship, and cannot easily access what Illich called 'vernacular values' or common sense, which can help to play down symptoms, and reassure the individual that they are not ill. Tiredness, even when persistent, need not mean that the individual is suffering from ME/CFS. The lack of 'collective wisdom' and the influence of 'significant others' also makes people vulnerable to media health scares and the expansion of medical markets, whether commercial or charitable. Changes in social structure and relationships cut the 'feedback loops' that help people maintain a sense of well-being even in the face of distress. This chimes in with general sociological discussions of postmodern social life and its link with crucial changes in the economy, where greater insecurity and uncertainty prevail, leading to the 'corrosion of character' (Sennett 1999).

Other forms of analysis of health in society have drawn attention to the modern/postmodern tendency for disease and illness to take on a particular symbolic significance in everyday life, reinforcing the processes outlined by Shorter. Perhaps the most influential writer in this regard is Susan Sontag, who, in a series of essays from the late 1970s onwards, has advanced a trenchant cultural critique of the use of the language of disease in public and private discourse (Sontag 1979, 1988). The tendency, for example, to associate the term 'cancer' with a variety of social and political processes (inflation, war or crime) reflects, Sontag argues, 'our shallow attitude towards death . . . our inability to construct an advanced industrial society which properly regulates consumption, and our justified fears of the increasingly violent course of history' (Sontag 1979: 87–8). Health and illness, in such a society, take on a wide range of meanings, which go beyond our immediate bodily concerns.

The use of military metaphors in 'fighting' disease – seeing cancer, for example, as 'invasive', or a matter of 'defences', or as being fought 'heroically' – further mystifies the real character of such illness, and reduces the ability of lay people and patients to face up to them (though see Seale 2002 for a counter-argument). This metaphorical aspect of illness in society is particularly evident in the case of HIV/AIDS, where all manner of ideas concerning punishment and judgement 'from above' have been rehearsed. Sontag makes the point that the language of viruses, reinforced so dramatically with the advent of HIV/AIDS, has now, unsurprisingly, been connected with the transformations brought about by the computer age. The virus metaphor, especially when it is expressed in terms of being able to replicate or 'make new copies of itself', reinforces ideas of illness as being unpredictable and fearsome (Sontag 1988: 70). Here, too, metaphor has the effect of detracting from an adequate societal response, to either illness or technical change, couched in language expressing clearly the issues involved. The over-use of inappropriate metaphors acts as a social crutch on which we lean, but which stops us from standing on our own two feet and facing reality.

The moral edge behind critiques of writers such as Shorter and Sontag constitutes a challenge to both popular and sociological thought about health in the future – but there is also an implied further point. This is that postmodern preoccupations with health and illness (whether in terms of their pervasiveness at the experiential level, or in terms of their cultural significance in everyday language) express a growing *irrationality* in contemporary cultures. In a book which caused considerable controversy and conflict for its author, Showalter (1998) propounds such an argument with some force. This line of analysis goes further than that of either of the two authors discussed so far, in linking health-related issues with other areas of lay belief and action. Showalter argues that preoccupations with the body, exemplified in disorders such as ME/CFS or Gulf War Syndrome, are forms of 'hysteria', along with such social and psychological phenomena as 'recovered memory syndrome' and 'satanic ritual abuse', which are fuelled by the media giving credence to all manner of claims without serious consideration of their factual basis.

In so far as some of these disorders and phenomena seem particularly to affect women, Showalter also challenges feminist thought, which, she says, has sometimes given credence to ideas such as recovered memory or satanic abuse (Showalter 1998: 11). She argues, rather, for a focus on the needs of women which give rise to such 'therapeutic investments, sickness lifestyles, and emotional hystories' (p. 11). In this way the current tendency to emphasize personal narratives and subjective experience is taken to task, and, as with Sontag and Shorter, we are asked to distinguish between realities, metaphors and myths. Showalter argues that although many forms of personal narrative can be therapeutic in character, this is not always the case, and real harm can come from misplaced or irrational beliefs. Again, such cultural trends are seen as deflecting attention from facing up to the causes of distress in modern society and constructing an approach to health, as well as to 'social ills', based on evidence and rationality. Similar arguments can be advanced against some aspects of the widespread and irrational use of complementary medicines (Whyte 2003: 119–23).

If there is one idea that runs through each of the arguments summarized briefly above, it is the problematic character of individual beliefs and subjectivity. The desire to stress the rationality of lay thought in everyday life has to be balanced with a consideration of those elements which are more problematic. This poses particular difficulties for medical sociology, especially in its efforts to give voice to the layperson or patient. What is involved here is the recognition of the limits of subjectivity, yet without losing the readiness to listen and represent clearly the form and content of lay thought. Much of the contribution of sociological research in the health field, discussed at various points in this book, has been to demonstrate the value of lay thought, or patient experience. There is no reason for this to be discontinued or downplayed.

But the discussion above does point to the limits of lay thought, as well as to the cultural context of 'postmodern society' in which it is fashioned. There are two points that can be made here. The first is that the tendency to move from an emphasis on lay *beliefs* to one on lay *knowledge* is to court difficulties in tackling health in the future. Prior (2003), for example, has shown that lay knowledge about specific health disorders is often quite limited. His examination of lay thinking about conditions such as Alzheimer's disease or brain injury revealed considerable misunderstanding and ignorance of the facts. What lay people (or carers) know a great deal about, of course, is their own experience, and this can be invaluable in attempting to fashion a more responsive health care system. But this is not the same as saying that lay people are experts about disease – in fact, knowledge is often 'partial or restricted' (Prior 2003: 49). Prior also considers the example of immunization, which, as we have seen, has been of continuing concern. In a study of the reasons for older people refusing an annual 'flu jab', Prior found that some 'refusers' gave no reason of any kind, whereas others showed a lack of knowledge of 'risk assessment, the nature and effects of influenza or of the nature and effects of vaccination against the flu' (p. 51).

The second point is that lay beliefs about health and illness need to be set in their context, and not simply accepted as forms of subjective 'truth' – a difficult concept at the best of times. Personal narratives need interpreting and contextualizing, in order to understand what role they perform in everyday life, and what effects they have on others (Bury 2001). Sociological research on health, at the level of lay ideas and everyday experience, needs, therefore, to be based on good empirical evidence and sound theoretical reasoning. In this way the critiques of social and cultural trends surrounding and shaping health, of the kind provided by Shorter, Sontag and Showalter, can be evaluated against sound first-hand research. Again, this is likely to paint a somewhat more complex picture of health in the future than the cultural critics allow, but one which is more accurate perhaps, and more relevant to health in everyday settings.

Concluding Remark

The above considerations bring us back, finally, to the main themes of this book: namely, that health is a dynamic process, and that it contains 'attributional' and 'relational' elements. The changing patterns of health and illness discussed here relate to altered social circumstances and altering perceptions. What counted as being healthy 50 years ago would not be readily accepted today – hence, in part at least, the tendency for lay people to report symptoms that may have been hidden or downplayed in the past. At the same time, medical technologies and health care have transformed many conditions that were once fatal into disorders that can be ameliorated, if not cured. Some forms of cancer and heart disease are showing considerable improvements in this regard. Non-life-threatening conditions are also increasingly amenable to treatment. A simple example such as poor eyesight illustrates the point. Today in developed countries, conditions such as cataracts and glaucoma in later life can be successfully treated, and therefore good eyesight can be maintained over longer periods of life. Individual health status is linked in important ways to changing patterns of health care. A dynamic view of such issues brings together biography and history, and suggests that a lifecourse perspective will be of continuing relevance to both quantitative and qualitative sociological research on health in the future.

What has also been illustrated throughout this book is that health includes both attributional and relational elements. It is important to recognize that some forms of health disorders – what in Western thought have been referred to as disease – rest, at crucial points, on the distinction of pathology from normality and on the biological attributes of bodily systems. Without the idea of pathology, the 'brute facts' of diseases such as cancer, heart disease, arthritis and stroke could not be properly understood. Such diseases cannot adequately be seen simply as social constructs, however much they are shaped by social factors and (changing) medical thought. Indeed, a clear, stable definition of such diseases is essential to an understanding of their social patterning; without it no such understanding is possible. Much of what lies behind our notions of health refers to the pain and suffering caused by pathologies that cannot be relativized away. But health also contains a strong relational dimension, in at least two senses. The first is that health and illness are indeed socially patterned in significant ways and lie beyond immediate personal experience (Blaxter 2003: 70). The second is that much so-called ill health, apart from frank disease, lies on a continuum that makes it problematic and contestable. Much mental health (though not all) and many physical and psychosomatic disorders lie on such a continuum; how and whether they are seen as illnesses, and how and whether they are treated, depend on the social relations that surround them.

Thus, both attributional and relational views are needed for an adequate picture of health in the round, though at any one time, and for any one purpose, a particular approach will be the focus of attention. The dividing line between the two can obviously be challenged; hence the demand by some patients in the present period to have their disorders recognized as (objective) disease and not simply as (subjective) illness. Health and illness in the future are likely to remain controversial, as the tensions between attributional and relational dimensions are argued about. The value of medical sociology for understanding health in the future will lie in its continuing ability to provide good empirical evidence of what is going on in such circumstances and plausible and theoretically informed interpretations of its observations. It will also continue to contribute to the evaluation of medicine and health care, and their relationship to health and illness, in the future.

References

Abercrombie, N. 2004: *Sociology*. Cambridge: Polity.

Alaszewski, A. and Horlick-Jones, T. 2003: How can doctors communicate information about risk more effectively? *British Medical Journal*, 327: 728–31.

Andrews, A. and Jewson, N. 1993: Ethnicity and infant deaths: the implications of recent statistical evidence for materialist explanations. *Sociology of Health and Illness*, 15 (2): 137–56.

Annandale, E. 1998: *The Sociology of Health and Medicine: A Critical Introduction*. Cambridge: Polity.

Annandale, E. and Hunt, K. 2000: Gender inequalities in health: research at the crossroads. In E. Annandale and K. Hunt (eds), *Gender Inequalities in Health*, Buckingham: Open University Press, 1–35.

Arber, S. and Cooper, H. 1999: Gender difference in health in later life: the new paradox? *Social Science and Medicine*, 48: 61–76.

Arber, S. and Cooper, H. 2000: Gender and inequalities in health across the lifecourse. In E. Annandale and K. Hunt (eds), *Gender Inequalities in Health*, Buckingham: Open University Press, 123–49.

Arber, S. and Ginn, J. 1991: *Gender and Later Life: A Sociological Analysis of Resources and Constraints*. London: Sage.

Arber, S. and Ginn, J. 2004: Ageing and gender: diversity and change. In *Social Trends 34*, London: The Stationery Office, 1–14.

Arber, S. and Thomas, H. 2001: From women's health to a gender analysis of health. In W. C. Cockerham (ed.), *The Blackwell Companion to Medical Sociology*, Oxford: Blackwell, 94–113.

Armstrong, D. 2002: Clinical autonomy, individual and collective: the problem of changing doctors' behaviour. *Social Science and Medicine*, 55 (10): 1771–7.

Barker, D. J. P. 1998: *Mothers, Babies and Disease in Later Life*, 2nd edn. Edinburgh: Churchill Livingstone.

Barnes, C. and Mercer, G. 2003: *Disability*. Cambridge: Polity.

Bartley, M. 1985: Coronary heart disease and the public health 1850–1983. *Sociology of Health and Illness*, 7: 289–313.

Bartley, M., Sacker, A., Firth, D. and Fitzpatrick, R. 1999: Social position, social roles and women's health in England: changing relationships, 1984–1993. *Social Science and Medicine*, 48: 99–115.

Bendelow, G. and Williams, S. J. (eds) 1998: *Emotions in Social Life: Social Theories and Contemporary Issues*. London: Routledge.

Berkman, L. F., Glass, T., Brissette, I. and Seeman, T. E. 2000: From social integration to health: Durkheim in the new millennium. *Social Science and Medicine*, 51: 843–57.

Bifulco, A. and Moran, P. 1998: *Wednesday's Child: Research into Women's Neglect and Abuse in Childhood, and Adult Depression*. London: Routledge.

Black, D. 1994: *A Doctor Looks at Health Economics*. London: The Office of Health Economics.

Blane, D., Davey Smith, G. and Bartley, M. 1993: Social selection: what does it contribute to social class differences in health? *Sociology of Health and Illness*, 15: 2–15.

Blaxter, M. 1990: *Health and Lifestyles*. London: Routledge.

Blaxter, M. 1993: Why do the victims blame themselves? In A. Radley (ed.), *Worlds of Illness: Biographical and Cultural Perspectives on Health and Disease*, London: Routledge, 124–42.

Blaxter, M. 2003: Biology, social class and inequalities in health: their synthesis in 'health capital'. In S. J. Williams, L. Birke and G. A. Bendelow (eds), *Debating Biology: Sociological Reflections on Health, Medicine and Society*, London: Routledge, 69–83.

Blaxter, M. 2004: *Health*. Cambridge: Polity.

Bloor, M. 1995: A user's guide to contrasting theories of HIV-related risk behaviour. In J. Gabe (ed.), *Medicine, Health and Risk: Sociological Approaches*, Oxford: Blackwell, 19–30.

Brown, G. W. and Harris, T. 1978: *Social Origins of Depression*. London: Tavistock.

Bunker, J. 2001: *Medicine Matters After All: Measuring the Benefits of Medical Care, a Healthy Lifestyle and a Just Social Environment*. London: The Nuffield Trust.

Bury, M. 1988: Meanings at risk: the experience of arthritis. In R. Anderson and M. Bury (eds), *Living with Chronic Illness: The Experience of Patients and their Families*, London: Unwin Hyman, 89–116.

Bury, M. 1995: Ageing, gender and sociological theory. In S. Arber and J. Ginn (eds), *Connecting Ageing and Gender: A Sociological Approach*, Buckingham: Open University Press, 15–29.

Bury, M. 1996: Defining and researching disability: challenges and responses. In C. Barnes and G. Mercer (eds), *Exploring the Divide: Illness and Disability*, Leeds: The Disability Press, 17–38.

Bury, M. 1997: *Health and Illness in a Changing Society*. London: Routledge.

Bury, M. 1998: Postmodernity and health. In G. Scambler and P. Higgs (eds), *Modernity, Medicine and Health: Medical Sociology Towards 2000*, London: Routledge, 1–28.

Bury, M. 2000a: Health, ageing and the lifecourse. In S. J. Williams, J. Gabe and M. Calnan (eds), *Health, Medicine and Society: Key Theories, Future Agendas*, London: Routledge, 87–105.

Bury, M. 2000b: On chronic illness and disability. In C. E. Bird, P. Conrad and A. M. Fremont (eds), *Handbook of Medical Sociology*, 5th edn, Upper Saddle River, NJ: Prentice-Hall, 173–83.

Bury, M. 2001: Illness narratives: fact or fiction? *Sociology of Health and Illness*, 23 (3): 263–85.

Bury, M. 2004: Researching patient/professional interactions. *Journal of Health Services Research and Policy*, 9 (supplement 1): 48–54.

Bury, M. and Gabe, J. 1994: Television medicine: medical dominance or trial by media? In J. Gabe, D. Kelleher and G. Williams (eds), *Challenging Medicine*, London: Routledge, 65–83.

Bury, M. and Wadsworth, M. 2003: The 'biological clock'? Ageing, health and the body across the lifecourse. In S. J. Williams, L. Birke and G. A. Bendelow (eds), *Debating Biology: Sociological Reflections on Health, Medicine and Society*, London: Routledge, 109–19.

Busfield, J. 1996: *Men, Women and Madness: Understanding Gender and Mental Disorder*. Houndsmill, Basingstoke: Macmillan.

Busfield, J. 2000: Introduction: rethinking the sociology of mental health. *Sociology of Health and Illness*, 22 (5): 543–58.

Cant, S. and Sharma, U. 1999: *A New Medical Pluralism? Alternative Medicine, Doctors, Patients and the State*. London: UCL Press.

Chang, V. W. and Christakis, N. A. 2002: Medical modelling of obesity: a transition from action to experience in a 20th century American textbook. *Sociology of Health and Illness*, 24 (2): 151–77.

Charatan, F. 1998: US panel calls for research into effects of Ritalin. *British Medical Journal*, 317: 1545.

Charles, C., Gafni, A. and Whelan, T. 1997: Shared decision-making in the medical encounter: what does it mean? (or it takes at least two to tango). *Social Science and Medicine*, 44 (5): 681–92.

Charles, C., Gafni, A. and Whelan, T. 1999: Decision-making in the physician–patient encounter: revisiting the shared treatment decision-making model. *Social Science and Medicine*, 49: 651–61.

Charmaz, K. 2000: Experiencing chronic illness. In G. L. Albrecht, R. Fitzpatrick and S. C. Scrimshaw (eds), *The Handbook of Social Studies in Health and Medicine*, London and New York: Sage, 277–92.

Chou, S., Grossman, M. and Saffer, H. 2004: An economic analysis of adult obesity: results from the Behavioral Risk Factor Surveillance System. *Journal of Health Economics*, 23: 565–87.

Clarke, A. E., Mamo, L., Fishman, J. R., Shim, J. K. and Fosket, J. R. 2003: Biomedicalization: technoscientific transformations of health, illness and U.S. biomedicine. *American Sociological Review*, 68: 161–94.

Cochrane, A. 1972: *Effectiveness and Efficiency: Random Reflections on Health Services*. London: Nuffield Provincial Hospital Trust.

Connell, R. W. 2002: *Gender*. Cambridge: Polity.

Conrad, P. 1994: Wellness as virtue: morality and the pursuit of health. *Culture, Medicine and Psychiatry*, 18: 385–401.

Conrad, P. 2000: Medicalization, genetics and human problems. In C. E. Bird, P. Conrad and A. M. Fremont (eds), *Handbook of Medical Sociology*, 5th edn, Upper Saddle River, NJ: Prentice-Hall, 322–33.

Conrad, P. and Jacobson, H. T. 2003: Enhancing biology? Cosmetic surgery and breast augmentation. In S. J. Williams, L. Birke and G. A. Bendelow (eds), *Debating Biology: Sociological Reflections on Health, Medicine and Society*, London: Routledge, 223–34.

Cooper, R. and Stoflet, S. 2004: Diversity and consistency: the challenge of maintaining quality in a multidisciplinary workforce. *Journal of Health Services Research and Policy*, 9 (supplement 1): 39–47.

Coulter, A. 1999: Paternalism or partnership? Patients have grown up – and there's no going back. *British Medical Journal*, 319: 719–20.

Coulter, A. 2002: *The Autonomous Patient: Ending Paternalism in Medical Care*. London: The Nuffield Trust/The Stationery Office.

Coulter, A. and Fitzpatrick, R. 2000: The patient's perspective regarding appropriate health care. In G. L. Albrecht, R. Fitzpatrick, and S. C. Scrimshaw (eds), *The Handbook of Social Studies in Health and Medicine*, London and New York: Sage, 454–64.

Craib, I. 1995: Some comments on the sociology of the emotions. *Sociology*, 29 (1): 151–8.

Crawford, R. 1980: Healthism and the medicalisation of everyday life. *International Journal of Health Services*, 19: 365–88.

Crossley, N. 2001: Embodiment and social structure: a response to Howson and Inglis. *The Sociological Review*, 49 (3): 318–26.

Davison, C., Frankel, S. and Davey Smith, G. 1992: The limits of popular lifestyle: reassign 'fatalism' in the popular culture of illness prevention. *Social Science and Medicine*, 34 (6): 675–85.

Davison, C., Davey Smith, G. and Frankel, S. 1991: Lay epidemiology and the prevention paradox: the implications of coronary candidacy for health promotion. *Sociology of Health and Illness*, 13 (1): 1–19.

Dingwall, R. 2002: Bioethics. In A. Pilnick, *Genetics and Society: An Introduction*, Buckingham: Open University Press, 161–80.

Dingwall, R., Fenn, P. and Quam, L. 1991: *Medical Negligence: A Review and Bibliography*. Oxford: Centre for Socio-Legal Studies, Wolfson College.

Dixon, A. et al. 2003: *Is the NHS Equitable?: A Review of the Evidence*. LSE Health and Social Care Discussion Paper Number 11. London: London School of Economic and Political Science.

DoH 2001: *Report of the Public Inquiry into Children's Heart Surgery at the Bristol Royal Infirmary 1984–1985*. Cmnd 5207. London: HMSO.

Doll, R. 1998: Controlled trials: the 1948 watershed. *British Medical Journal*, 317: 1217–20.

Donaldson, L. 2003: Expert patients usher in a new era of opportunity for the NHS. *British Medical Journal*, 326: 1279–80.

Doran, T., Drever, F. and Whitehead, M. 2004: Is there is north–south divide in social class inequalities in health in Great Britain? Cross-sectional study using data from the 2001 census. *British Medical Journal*, 328: 1043–5.

Double, D. 2002: The limits of psychiatry. *British Medical Journal*, 321: 900–4.

Doust, J. 2004: Why do doctors use treatments that do not work? *British Medical Journal*, 328: 474–5.

Doyal, L. 1995: *What Makes Women Sick: Gender and the Political Economy of Health*. London: Macmillan.

Drever, F. and Whitehead, M. 1997: *Health Inequalities*. London: The Stationery Office.

Eaton, L. 2002: A third of Europeans and almost half of Americans use the Internet for health information. *British Medical Journal*, 325: 989.

Ebrahim, S. 2002: The medicalisation of old age – should be encouraged. *British Medical Journal*, 324: 861–3.

Estes, C. L., Wallace, S. and Linkins, K. W. 2000: Political economy of health and aging. In C. E. Bird, P. Conrad and A. M. Fremont (eds), *Handbook of Medical Sociology*, 5th edn, Upper Saddle River, NJ: Prentice-Hall, 129–42.

Fabrega, H. Jr and Manning, P. 1973: An integrated theory of disease: Ladino–Mestizo views of disease in Chiapos Highlands. *Psychosomatic Medicine*, 35 (3): 223–39.

Faris, R. E. L. and Dunham, H. W. 1965 [1939]: *Mental Disorders in Urban Areas*. Chicago: University of Chicago Press.

Featherstone, K. and Donovan, J. L. 2002: 'Why don't they just tell me straight, why allocate it?' The struggle to make sense of participating in a randomised controlled trial. *Social Science and Medicine*, 55 (5): 709–19.

Fitzpatrick, R. 2004: Evaluation. In J. Gabe, M. Bury and M. A. Elston (eds), *Key Concepts in Medical Sociology*, London: Sage, 247–52.

Foucault, M. 1967: *Madness and Civilization*. London: Tavistock.

Foucault, M. 1973: *The Birth of the Clinic*. London: Tavistock.

Frank, A. W. 1991: *At the Will of the Body: Reflections on Illness*. Boston and New York: Houghton Mifflin.

Frank, A. W. 1995: *The Wounded Storyteller: Body, Illness and Ethics*. Chicago: University of Chicago Press.

Freidson, E. 1970/1988: *Profession of Medicine: A Study of the Sociology of Applied Knowledge*. Chicago: University of Chicago Press.

Freidson, E. 2001: *Professionalism: The Third Logic*. Cambridge: Polity.

French, S. 1993: Disability, impairment or something in between? In J. Swain, V. Finkelstein, S. French and M. Oliver (eds), *Disabling Barriers – Enabling Environments*, London: Sage in association with the Open University, 17–25.

Freund, P. E. S., McGuire, M. B. and Podhurst, L. S. 2003: *Health, Illness and the Social Body: A Critical Sociology*, 4th edn. Upper Saddle River, NJ: Prentice-Hall.

Gabe, J. 2004: Managerialism. In J. Gabe, M. Bury and M. A. Elston (eds), *Key Concepts in Medical Sociology*, London: Sage, 212–17.

Gabe, J., Olumide, G. and Bury, M. 2004: 'It takes three to tango': a framework for understanding patient partnership in paediatric clinics. *Social Science and Medicine*, 59: 1071–9.

Gerhardt, U. 1989: *Ideas about Illness: An Intellectual and Political History of Medical Sociology*. London: Macmillan.

Giddens, A. 1991: *Modernity and Self-Identity: Self and Society in the Late Modern Age*. Cambridge: Polity.

Goffman, I. 1963a: *Behaviour in Public Places*. Harmondsworth: Penguin Books.

Goffman, I. 1963b: *Stigma: Notes on the Management of Spoiled Identity*. Harmondsworth: Penguin Books.

Goffman, I. 1971: The insanity of place. In I. Goffman, *Relations in Public*, Harmondsworth: Pelican Books, 389–450.

Gove, W. 1974: Individual resources and mental hospitalisation: a comparison and evaluation of societal reaction and psychiatric perspectives. *American Sociological Review*, 39: 86–100.

Gravelle, H., Wildman, J. and Sutton, M. 2002: Income, income inequality and health: what can we learn from aggregate data? *Social Science and Medicine*, 54: 577–89.

Gray, A. (ed.) 2001: *World Health and Disease*. Buckingham: Open University Press.

Hafner, H. and an der Heiden, W. 1997: Epidemiology of schizophrenia. *Canadian Journal of Psychiatry*, 47 (March): 139–51.

Ham, C., York, N., Sutch, S. and Shaw, R. 2003: Hospital bed utilisation in the NHS, Kaiser Permanente, and the US Medicare programme: analysis of routine data. *British Medical Journal*, 327: 1257–60.

Hansen, M., Kurinczuk, J. J., Bower, C. and Webb, S. 2002: The risk of major birth defects after intracytoplasmic sperm injection and in vitro fertilization. *New England Journal of Medicine*, 346: 725–30.

Hardey, M. 1999: Doctor in the house: the Internet as a source of lay health knowledge and a challenge to expertise. *Sociology of Health and Illness*, 21 (6): 820–35.

Healy, D. 1999: *The Antidepressant Era*. Cambridge, Mass., and London: Harvard University Press.

Herzlich, C. 1973: *Health and Illness: A Social Psychological Analysis*. London: Academic Press.

Hollingshead, A. B. and Redlich, F. C. 1958: *Social Class and Mental Illness*. New York: Wiley.

Howard, M. 2002: *The Invention of Peace and the Reinvention of War*. London: Profile Books.

Howitt, A. and Armstrong, D. 1999: Implementing evidence-based medicine in general practice. *British Medical Journal*, 318: 1324–7.

Howson, A. and Inglis, D. 2001: The body in sociology: tensions inside and outside sociological thought. *The Sociological Review*, 49 (3): 297–317.

Jamieson, L. 1997: *Intimacy: Personal Relationships in Modern Societies*. Cambridge: Polity.

Joshi, H., Wiggins, R. D., Bartley, M., Mitchell, R., Gleave, S. and Lynch, K. 2000: Putting health inequalities on the map: does where you live matter and why? In H. Graham (ed.), *Understanding Health Inequalities*, Buckingham: Open University Press, 143–55.

Judge, K., Mulligan, J. and Benzeval, M. 1998: Income inequality and population health. *Social Science and Medicine*, 46: 567–79.

Karlsen, S. and Nazroo, J. Y. (2002) Agency and structure: the impact of ethnic identity and racism on the health of ethnic minority people. *Sociology of Health and Illness*, 24 (1): 1–20.

Karpf, A. 1988: *Doctoring the Media: Reporting of Health and Medicine*. London: Routledge.

Katz, S. 1996: *Disciplining Old Age: The Formation of Gerontological Knowledge*. Charlottesville and London: University Press of Virginia.

Kelleher, D. and Hillier, S. (eds) 1996: *Researching Cultural Differences in Health*. London: Routledge.

Kelly, M. and Field, D. 1996: Medical sociology, chronic illness and the body. *Sociology of Health and Illness*, 18 (2): 241–57.

Kennedy, A., Gately, C. and Rogers, A. 2004: *Assessing the Process of Embedding EPP in the NHS: Preliminary Survey of PCT Pilot Schemes*. Manchester: National Primary Care Research and Development Team.

Kleinman, A. 1988: *The Illness Narratives: Suffering, Healing and the Human Condition*. New York: Basic Books.

Kuh, D. and Wadsworth, M. E. J. 1989: Parental height, childhood environment and subsequent adult height in a national birth cohort. *International Journal of Epidemiology*, 18: 663–8.

Lancet 2003: MMR vaccination: a no brainer? *The Lancet*, 362 (1 Nov.).

Law, C. M. 1994: Employment and industrial structure. In J. Obelkevich and P. Catterall (eds), *Understanding Post-War British Society*, London and New York: Routledge, 85–98.

Lawrence, C. 1995: *Medicine in the Making of Modern Britain 1700–1920*. London: Routledge.

Leon, D. A., Lithell, H. O., Vågerö, D., Koupilová, I., Mohsen, R., Berglund, L., Lithell, U. B. and McKeigue, P. M. 1998: Reduced fetal growth rate and increased risk of death from ischaemic heart disease: cohort study of 15,000 Swedish men and women born 1915–29. *British Medical Journal*, 317: 241–5.

Link, B. G. and Phelan, J. C. 2000: Evaluating the fundamental cause explanation for social determinants of health. In C. E. Bird, P. Conrad and A. M. Fremont (eds), *Handbook of Medical Sociology*, 5th edn, Upper Saddle River, NJ: Prentice-Hall, 33–46.

Littlewood, R. and Lipsedge, M. 1997: *Aliens and Alienists: Ethnic Minorities and Psychiatry*, 3rd edn. London: Routledge.

Lockyer, L. and Bury, M. 2002: The construction of a modern epidemic: the implications for women of the gendering of coronary heart disease. *Journal of Advanced Nursing*, 39 (5): 432–40.

Lorber, J. 2000: Gender and health. In P. Brown (ed.), *Perspectives in Medical Sociology*, 3rd edn, Prospect Heights, Ill.: Waveland Press, 40–70.

Lorig, K. R., Sobel, D. S., Stewart, A. L., Brown, B. W. Jr, Bandura, A., Ritter, P., Gonzalez, V. M., Laurent, D. D. and Holman, H. R. 1999: Evidence suggesting that a chronic disease self-management program can improve health status while reducing hospitalisation: a randomised trial. *Medical Care*, 37 (1): 5–14.

Lynch, J., Davey Smith, G., Hillemeier, M., Shaw, M., Raghunathan, T. and Kaplan, G. 2001: Income inequality, the psychosocial environment, and health: comparisons of wealthy nations. *The Lancet*, 358: 194–200.

Lynch, J. W., Smith, G. D., Kaplan, G. A. and House, J. S. 2000: Income inequality and mortality: importance to health of individual income, psychosocial environment, or material conditions. *British Medical Journal*, 320: 1200–4.

Macintyre, S., Ellaway, A. and Cummins, S. 2002: Place effects on health: how can we conceptualise, operationalise and measure them? *Social Science and Medicine*, 55: 125–39.

Macintyre, S., Ford, G. and Hunt, K. 1999: Do women 'over-report' morbidity? Men's and women's responses to structured prompting on a standard questionnaire on long-standing illness. *Social Science and Medicine*, 48: 89–98.

Macintyre, S., Hunt, K. and Sweeting, H. 1996: Gender difference in health: are things as simple as they seem? *Social Science and Medicine*, 42 (4): 617–24.

Mackenbach, J. P. and Bakker, M. J. 2003: Tackling socio-economic inequalities in health: analysis of European experiences. *The Lancet*, 362: 1409–14.

Manton, K. and Gu, X. 2001: Changes in the prevalence of chronic disability in the United States black and non black population above age 65 from 1982 to 1999. *Proceedings of the National Academy of Science*, 98 (11): 6354–9.

Marmot, M. 1989: General approaches to migrant studies: the relation between disease, social class and ethnic origin. In J. Cruickshank and D. Beevers (eds), *Ethnic Factors in Health and Disease*, Sevenoaks: Wright, 12–17.

Marmot, M. 1998: The magnitude of social inequalities is coronary heart disease: possible explanations. In I. Sharp (ed.), *Social Inequalities in Heart Disease Opportunities for Action*, National Heart Forum, London: The Stationary Office, 19–30.

Marmot, M. 1999: Introduction. In M. Marmot and R. G. Wilkinson (eds), *Social Determinants of Health*, Oxford: Oxford University Press, 1–16.

Marmot, M. 2003: Self esteem and health. *British Medical Journal*, 327: 574–5.

Marmot, M. 2004: *Status Syndrome: How Your Social Standing Directly Affects Your Health and Life Expectancy*. London: Bloomsbury.

Marmot, M. and Wilkinson, R. G. 2001: Psychosocial and material pathways in the relation between income and health: a response to Lynch et al. *British Medical Journal*, 322: 1233–6.

Marmot, M., Davey Smith, G., Stansfeld, S., Patel, C., North, F., Head, J., White, I., Brunner, E. and Feeney, A. 1991: Health inequalities among British civil servants: the Whitehall II study. *The Lancet*, 337: 1387–93.

Marmot, M., Rose, G., Shipley, M. and Hamilton, P. 1978: Employment grade and coronary heart disease in British civil servants. *Journal of Epidemiology and Community Health*, 32: 244–9.

Mayor, S. 2001: Health department to fund interferon despite institute's ruling. *British Medical Journal*, 323: 1087.

McKeown, T. 1979: *The Role of Medicine: Dream, Mirage or Nemesis?* Oxford: Blackwell.

McKinlay, J. B. and Marceau, L. D. 2002: The end of the golden age of doctoring. *International Journal of Health Services*, 32 (2): 379–416.

Mead, N., Varnam, R., Rogers, A. and Roland, M. 2003: What predicts patient's interest in the Internet as a health resource in health care in England? *Journal of Health Services Research and Policy*, 8 (1): 33–9.

Morris, J. N. 1975: *The Uses of Epidemiology*, 3rd edn. Edinburgh: Churchill Livingstone.

Moynihan, R. and Smith, R. 2002: Too much medicine? Almost certainly. *British Medical Journal*, 324: 859–60.

Nazroo, J. 1997a: *Ethnicity and Mental Health*. London: Policy Studies Institute.

Nazroo, J. 1997b: *The Health of Britain's Ethnic Minorities*. London: Policy Studies Institute.

Nettleton, S. and Watson, J. (eds) 1998: *The Body in Everyday Life*. London: Routledge.

NICE 2000: Guidance on the use of methylphenidate (Ritalin, Equasym) for attention deficit/hyperactivity disorder (ADHD) in childhood. London: National Institute for Clinical Excellence.

Oakley, A. 1984: *The Captured Womb: A History of the Medical Care of Pregnant Women*. Oxford: Blackwell.

Oliver, M. 1990: *The Politics of Disablement*. Basingstoke: Macmillan.

Oliver, M. 1996: *Understanding Disability: From Theory to Practice.* Basingstoke: Macmillan.

ONS 2002: *Social Trends No. 32.* London: The Stationery Office.

ONS 2004: *Social Trends No. 34.* London: The Stationary Office.

Parens, E. and Knowles, L. P. 2003: *Reprogenetics and Public Policy: Reflections and Recommendations.* New York: Hastings Center.

Parsons, E. and Atkinson, P. 1992: Lay constructions of genetic risk. *Sociology of Health and Illness*, 14 (4): 437–55.

Pilnick, A. 2002: *Genetics and Society: An Introduction.* Buckingham: Open University Press.

Popay, J. and Groves, K. 2000: 'Narrative' in research on gender inequalities in health. In E. Annandale and K. Hunt (eds), *Gender Inequalities in Health*, Buckingham: Open University Press, 64–89.

Porter, R. 1997: *The Greatest Benefit to Mankind: A Medical History of Humanity from Antiquity to the Present.* London: Harper Collins.

Porter, R. 2002a: *Blood and Guts: A Short History of Medicine.* London: Allen Lane.

Porter, R. 2002b: *Madness: A Brief History.* Oxford: Oxford University Press.

Prentice, A. M. and Jebb, S. A. 1995: Obesity in Britain, gluttony or sloth? *British Medical Journal*, 311: 437–9.

Prior, L. 2003: Belief, knowledge and expertise: the emergence of the lay expert in medical sociology. *Sociology of Health and Illness*, 25 (Silver Anniversary Issue): 41–57.

Rawlins, M. D. 2001: The failings of NICE. *British Medical Journal*, 322: 489.

Riley, M. W., Foner, A. and Waring, J. 1988: Sociology on age. In N. J. Smelser (ed.), *Handbook of Sociology*, London and Newbury Park: Sage, 243–90.

Rogers, A. and Pilgrim, D. 2003: *Mental Health and Inequality.* Houndsmill, Basingstoke: Palgrave Macmillan.

Rogers, A., Hassell, K. and Nicolas, G. 1999: *Demanding Patients? Analysing the Use of Primary Care.* Buckingham: Open University Press.

Sacker, A., Firth, D., Fitzpatrick, R., Lynch, K. and Bartley, M. 2000: Comparing health inequality in men and women: prospective study of mortality 1986–96. *British Medical Journal*, 320: 1303–7.

Sackett, D. L., Rosenberg, W. M. C., Gray, M. J. A., Haynes, R. B. and Richardson, W. S. 1996: Evidence based medicine: what it is and what it isn't. *British Medical Journal*, 312: 71–2.

Sanders, C., Donovan, J. and Dieppe, P. 2002: The significance and consequences of having painful and disabling joints in older age: co-existing accounts of normal and disrupted biographies. *Sociology of Health and Illness*, 24 (2): 227–53.

Scheff, T. 1999 [1967]: *Being Mentally Ill: A Sociological Theory*, 3rd edn. New York: de Gruyter.

Seale, C. 2002: Cancer heroics: a study of news reports with particular reference to gender. *Sociology*, 36 (1): 107–26.

Sen, A. 2002: Health: perception versus observation. *British Medical Journal*, 324: 860–1.

Sennett, R. 1999: *The Corrosion of Character: The Personal Consequences of Work in the New Capitalism*. New York: Norton.

Sennett, R. 2003: *Respect in a World of Inequality*. New York: Norton.

Shakespeare, T. 1999: Losing the plot? Medical and activist discourses of contemporary genetics and disability. *Sociology of Health and Illness*, 21 (5): 669–88.

Shakespeare, T. 2003: Rights, risks and responsibilities: new genetics and disabled people. In S. J. Williams, J. Gabe and M. Calnan (eds), *Health, Medicine and Society: Key Theories, Future Agendas*, London: Routledge, 198–209.

Shilling, C. 1993/2003: *The Body and Social Theory*. London: Sage.

Shilling, C. 2001: Embodiment, experience and theory: in defence of the sociological tradition. *The Sociological Review*, 49 (3): 327–44.

Shilling, C. 2002: Culture, the 'sick role' and the consumption of health. *British Journal of Sociology*, 53 (4): 621–38.

Shorter, E. 1993: *From Paralysis to Fatigue: History of Psychosomatic Illness in the Modern Era*. New York: Free Press.

Showalter, E. 1998: *Hystories: Hysterical Epidemics and Modern Culture*. London: Picador.

Silverman, D. 1987: *Communication and Medical Practice: Social Relations in the Clinic*. London: Sage.

Smaje, C. 1996: The ethnic patterning of health: new directions for theory and research. *Sociology of Health and Illness*, 18 (2): 139–71.

Smaje, C. 2000: Race, ethnicity, and health. In C. E. Bird, P. Conrad, and A. M. Fremont (eds), *Handbook of Medical Sociology*, 5th edn, Upper Saddle River, NJ: Prentice-Hall, 114–28.

Smith, R. 2000: The failings of NICE. *British Medical Journal*, 311: 3264.

Smith, R. 2002: The discomfort of patient power. *British Medical Journal*, 324: 497–8.

Sontag, S. 1979: *Illness as Metaphor*. London: Allen Lane.

Sontag, S. 1988: *Aids and its Metaphors*. Harmondsworth: Penguin Books.

Stimson, G. 1974: Obeying doctor's orders: a view from the other side. *Social Science and Medicine*, 8: 97–104.

Stimson, G. and Webb, B. 1975: *Going to See the Doctor: The Consultation Process in General Practice*. London: Routledge and Kegan Paul.

Strong, P. 1979: *The Ceremonial Order of the Clinic: Parent, Doctors and Medical Bureaucracies*. London: Routledge and Kegan Paul.

Szreter, S. 2001: The importance of social intervention in Britain's mortality decline c.1850–1914: a reinterpretation of the role of public health. In B. Davey, A. Gray and C. Seale (eds), *Health and Disease: A Reader*, 3rd edn, Buckingham: Open University Press, 219–26.

Thomas, C. 1999: *Female Forms: Experiencing and Understanding Disability*. Buckingham: Open University Press.

Townsend, P. and Davidson, N. 1992: *Inequalities in Health: The Black Report*. Harmondsworth: Penguin Books.

Turner, B. S. 1996: *The Body and Society: Explorations in Social Theory*, 2nd edn. London: Sage.

Vågerö, D. and Illsley, R. 1995: Explaining health inequalities: beyond Black and Barker. *European Sociological Review*, 11 (3): 219–41.

Wadsworth, M. 1991: *The Imprint of Time: Childhood, History and Adult Life*. Oxford: Oxford University Press.

Wadsworth, M. 1997: Health inequalities in the lifecourse perspective. *Social Science and Medicine*, 44 (6): 859–69.

Wadsworth, M. 1999: Early life. In M. Marmot and R. G. Wilkinson (eds), *Social Determinants of Health*, Oxford: Oxford University Press, 44–63.

Wakefield, A. J., Murch, S. H., Anthony, A., Linnell, J., Casson, D. M., Malik, M., Berelowitz, M., Dhillon, A. P., Thomson, M. A., Harvey, P., Valentine, A., Davies, S. E. and Walker-Smith, J. A. 1998: Ileal-lymphoid-nodular hyperpalsia, non-specific colitis, and pervasive developmental disorder in children. *The Lancet*, 351: 637–41.

Waldron, I. 2000: Trends in gender difference in mortality: relationships to changing gender differences in behaviour and other causal factors. In E. Annandale and K. Hunt (eds), *Gender Inequalities in Health*, Buckingham: Open University Press, 150–81.

Waldron, I. 2001: What do we know about causes of sex differences in mortality? A review of the literature? In P. Conrad (ed.), *The Sociology of Health and Illness: Critical Perspectives*, 6th edn, New York: Worth, 37–49.

Webster, C. 1994: Tuberculosis. In C. Seale and S. Pattison (eds), *Medical Knowledge: Doubt and Certainty*, Buckingham: Open University Press, 36–59.

Whitehead, M. 1992: *The Health Divide*. Harmondsworth: Penguin Books.

Whitehead, M., Diderichsen, F. and Burstrom, B. 2000: Researching the impact of public policy on inequalities in health. In H. Graham (ed.), *Understanding Health Inequalities*, Buckingham: Open University Press, 203–18.

Wholey, D. R. and Burns, L. R. 2000: Tides of change: the evolution of managed care in the United States. In C. E. Bird, P. Conrad and A. M. Fremont (eds), *Handbook of Medical Sociology*, 5th edn. Upper Saddle River, NJ: Prentice-Hall, 217–37.

Whyte, J. 2003: *Bad Thoughts: A Guide to Clear Thinking*. London: Corvo Books.

Wilkinson, R. G. 1996: *Unhealthy Societies: The Afflictions of Inequality*. London: Routledge.

Wilkinson, R. G. 2004: The epidemiological transition: from material scarcity to social disadvantage. In M. Bury and J. Gabe (eds), *The Soci-*

ology of Health and Illness: A Reader, London: Routledge, 112–21 (first published in *Daedalus*, 123 (4) (1994): 61–77).

Williams, D. 2000: Race, SES, and health: the added effects of racism and discrimination. In P. Brown (ed.), *Perspectives in Medical Sociology*, 3rd edn, Prospect Heights, Ill.: Waveland Press, 21–39.

Williams, G. 1984: The genesis of chronic illness: narrative reconstruction. *Sociology of Health and Illness*, 6 (2): 175–200.

Williams, G. 1998: The sociology of disability: towards a materialist phenomenology. In T. Shakespeare (ed.), *The Disability Reader: Social Science Perspectives*, London Cassell, 234–44.

Williams, G. 2001: Theorising disability. In G. L. Albrecht, K. Seelman and M. Bury (eds), *Handbook of Disability Studies*, Thousand Oaks, Calif. and London: Sage, 123–44.

Williams, S. J. and Calnan, M. (eds) 1996: *Modern Medicine: Lay Perspectives and Experiences*. London: UCL Press.

Wilson, P. M. 2001: A policy analysis of the Expert Patient in the United Kingdom: self-care as an expression of pastoral power? *Health and Social Care in the Community*, 9 (3): 134–42.

Zola, I. 1972: Medicine as an institution of social control. *Sociological Review*, 20: 487–504.

Zola, I. 1993: Self, identity and the naming question: reflections on the language of disability. *Social Science and Medicine*, 36: 167–73.

Index

Breinigsville, PA USA
07 December 2010
0866BV00002B/1/P